"We did not inherit the earth from our parents. We are borrowing it from our children." —Native American saying

This book was made possible through the generosity of

 Eastman Kodak Company

"If there is magic on this planet,

it is contained in water. . . . Its

substance reaches everywhere; it

touches the past and prepares the

future; it moves under the poles

and wanders thinly in the heights

of air. It can assume forms of

exquisite perfection in a snowflake,

or strip the living to a single

shining bone cast up by the sea."

—*Loren Eiseley*

"*This grand show is eternal.*

It is always sunrise somewhere:

the dew is never all dried at once:

a shower is forever falling, vapor

is ever rising. Eternal sunrise,

eternal sunset, eternal dawn and

gloaming, on sea and continents

and islands, each in its turn, as the

round earth rolls." —*John Muir*

"The earth does not belong to

man; man belongs to the earth.

This we know. All things are

connected like the blood which

unites one family. All things are

connected." —Chief Seattle

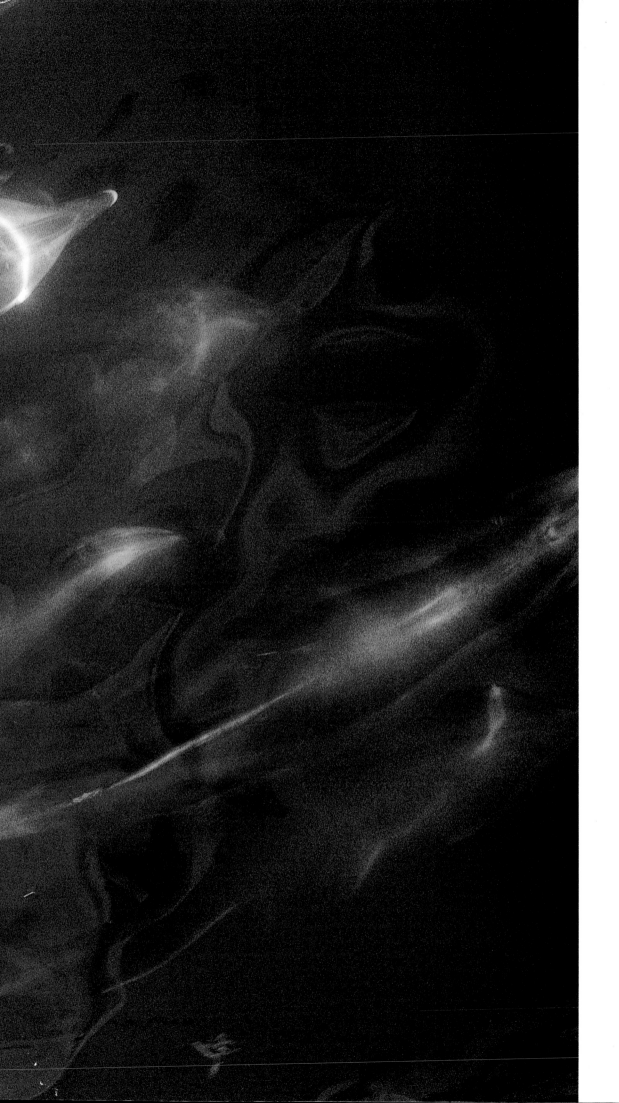

"Nature may be compared to a vast ocean. Thousands and millions of changes are taking place in it. Crocodiles and fish are essentially of the same substance as the water in which they live. Man is crowded together with the myriad other things in the Great Changingness, and his nature is one with that of all other natural things."

—T'ien T'ung-Hsu

"*The first day or so we all pointed to our countries. The third or fourth day we were pointing to our continents. By the fifth day we were aware of only one Earth.*"

—*Sultan Bin Salman al-Saud, astronaut*

Page 1: Earth, Crescent, Apollo 12: Photo by: NASA JSC/Starlight
Page 2: Calley Glacier, Antarctic: Photo by: Gordon Wiltsie
Page 4: Borneo, Malaysia: Mulu National Park, threatened by
commercial deforestation, may now be saved as an international
biosphere reserve. Photo by: John Werner
Page 6: Roraima, Brazil: Yanomami swimmers. Photo by: Claus Meyer
Page 8: Baja, California: Bottlenose dolphins. Photo by: Kevin Schafer
Page 10: Oahu, Hawaii, USA: Highway through the Koolau Range.
Photo by: Paul Chesley/Photographers/Aspen

First published in 1990 by Collins Publishers San Francisco
A Division of HarperCollinsPublishers

Copyright © 1990 by Collins Publishers

Library of Congress Cataloging-in-Publication Data:
ISBN 0-00-637660-6
1. Pollution–Pictorial works.
2. Man–Influence on nature–Pictorial works.
I. Title

TD174.B76 1990   *90-40959*
363.73'022'2–dc20   *CIP*

Printed in Japan
First printing August 1990   *10 9 8 7 6 5 4 3 2 1*

ONE EARTH

*Photographed by more than
80 of the world's leading photojournalists*

*Written by Kenneth Brower
Introduction by Michael Tobias*

Collins Publishers San Francisco
A Division of HarperCollins*Publishers*

"Photography is a small voice, at best, but sometimes—just sometimes—one photograph or a group of them can lure our senses into awareness." —W. Eugene Smith

Since the first stirrings of civilization, human beings have taken the earth's gifts. We have plowed earth's fertile soil, harvested its bounty, delighted in its benevolence and extolled its infinite beauty and goodness. "One generation passeth away, and another generation cometh," wrote the ancient poet Ecclesiastes, "but the earth abideth forever."

After thousands of years, that faith in the earth's durability is finally being called into question. For all of the earth's seemingly endless gifts, it is clear that the natural world is not invincible. Like other living things, it is vulnerable, needy and moody. And its fragility is a direct result of human activity.

While we have enjoyed our planet, we have also abused it. Civilization has brought with it all manner of ecological trespass. We have mined earth's minerals, dumped in its waters, cut down forests and filled the air with fumes. On the slopes of Mount Everest, even in the ice of Antarctica, we have left our imprint on once-pristine wilderness.

Henry David Thoreau wrote more than a century ago that "in wildness is the preservation of the world." Fortunately for the earth's survival, increasing numbers of people are realizing that we disregard nature at our peril. Today, three-quarters of all Americans describe themselves as environmentalists. Polls in Europe and parts of Asia hint at even higher percentages. No religion, no political sentiment, has ever claimed such a following. We may well be at a planetary turning point.

Some of these environmentalists devote their lives to lobbying and preservation. Others consider themselves environmentalists because they recycle their newspapers and try to conserve resources. And some of the most important environmental work is being done by people who don't identify themselves as environmentalists: individuals whose lives are directly affected by pollution and have taken steps to clean up their communities. People around the world are beginning to understand the meaning of stewardship: taking only what is needed, leaving the rest intact.

Photojournalism has a unique role to play in raising an ecological consciousness. W. Eugene Smith, a legendary photojournalist, once wrote: "Photography is a small voice, at best, but sometimes–just sometimes–one photograph or a group of them can lure our senses into awareness." That has been the goal of *One Earth*. For this book, more than 80 of the world's leading photojournalists spread out across the continents. Because the earth's condition is so much a by-product of human activities, they focused on people interacting with nature, for better or worse. The result is a rare family portrait.

This book does not avoid ugly truths. We see tropical wastelands, bayous pervaded by petrochemicals, devastated wildlife and toxic hotspots. We encounter human overcrowding, hunger and disease. But where there is horror, there is also hope.

The same photographic sensibility that identifies destruction also seeks out celebration, initiative and invention. Renewal reveals itself in urban gardens, protests against hazardous waste, tree plantings in the desert, recycling of society's detritus and tender care for struggling species. Solutions can be–in fact, need to be–both local and global.

There is, indeed, only one earth–and it is an interdependent place. Sulphur dioxide emissions from factories in the United States turn to acid rain that destroys maple trees in Canada. A nuclear plant implodes in Chernobyl, and the reindeer herds in Lapland become radioactive. Fast-food restaurants in the northern hemisphere demand beef, and ranchers cut down tropical rainforest to raise cattle. Smog is not a phenomenon of one unfortunate metropolis, but occurs everywhere that car and industrial emissions exceed the atmosphere's ability to absorb them.

There are four billion more people alive today than during the 1850s and '60s, when photojournalism got its start. Back then, photographers like Mathew Brady and Carleton Watkins covered the carnage of the Civil War and the splendors of the newly-discovered Yosemite Valley. Today's wilderness is not quite the exotic "other" it used to be. We can no longer afford to perceive the plights of distant lands and cultures as unconnected to ourselves.

One Earth's photographers have captured a living planet, a small blue miracle drifting discreetly in one corner of the Milky Way. They detail exquisite beauty and warn us of pressing problems. Just as importantly, they offer hope. The human race is rallying. The earth desperately needs the personal help and restraint of each of us. *—Michael Tobias*

"For the sea lies all about us....

In its mysterious past it encompasses

all the dim origins of life and

receives in the end, after, it may

be, many transmutations, the

dead husks of that same life.

For all at last returns to the sea—

to Oceanus, the ocean river,

like the overflowing stream of

time, the beginning and the end."

—Rachel Carson

◄ **Falkland Islands:** (previous page) Gentoo penguins are the marines of the Southern Ocean, an honor guard for Antarctica and the best-loved symbols of that last wild continent. They are sharp in their uniforms, but no longer quite immaculate. During the 1970s, scientists found residues of the pesticide DDT in penguin fat. Antarctica, we had thought, was pristine. It was the most remote continent, biologically isolated from other mainlands by the ice and gales of the Southern Ocean. DDT was never sprayed there: no pests, no need. Yet there it was, DDT, concentrated in the fat of

penguins. No corner of the planet, it seems, is safe from our mistakes. *Photo by: Frans Lanting/ Minden Pictures*

◄ **Shasta County, California, USA:** Burney Falls. Water gives us life and solace. "It was rare and comforting to waken late and hear the undiminished shouting of the water in the night," wrote novelist Wallace Stegner. "And at sunup it was still there, powerful and incessant, with the slant sun tangled in its rainbow spray, the grass blue with wetness, and the air heady as ether and scented with campfire smoke." *Photo by: David Cavagnaro/DRK Photo*

▲ **Venice, Italy:** Venice and all its architecture are under siege by the sea. St. Mark's Square is often flooded at high tide by a rising Adriatic–the result, some believe, of global warming. Engineers have designed a sea wall with flexible gates to try to hold back the water. *Photo by: Raphaël Gaillarde*

▶ **Okinawa, Japan:** Sea fans, a variety of gorgonian coral, spread at right angles to the current, feeding on plankton. Coral reefs have been called "the ultimate ecosystem." No biological community is more complex, save for tropical rainforest. The planet's reefs lie almost entirely in the tropics. Overfishing, quarrying of coral, deforestation and the consequent siltation of lagoons have caused extensive damage.

The news is not all bleak. Australia's Great Barrier Reef Marine Park protects the planet's largest reef and serves as a model for reef preservation everywhere. In the Philippines, an archipelago with the richest reef communities on earth, as well as the most damaged, several innovative programs have succeeded in persuading fishermen that conservation makes economic sense. There are new marine parks in Indonesia and Papua, New Guinea. For the otherworldly beauty of the reef, there is still hope. *Photo by: David Doubilet*

▲ **Homosassa Springs, Florida, USA:** Barbara Bernier, an animal behaviorist, confers with Sunrise, a young male manatee. "Manatees are slow, gentle creatures," she says. "They're unique in having no known natural predators and no prey. They have no fear of man, or boat, or anything else. It's like swimming with a puppy dog." There are only 1,000 to 1,500 left in Florida, and they are dying at the rate of about 100 a year from loss of habitat and collisions with boat propellers, as well as natural causes. *Photo by: Douglas Faulkner*

▶ **Seattle, Washington, USA:** Puget Sound is the least polluted major estuary of the lower 48 states. Its waters are shared by oil tankers, salmon and killer whales–proof that coexistence in the seas is possible. At the Seattle Aquarium's "Touch Tank," young visitors gain a feel for the sea. *Photo by: Peter Haley/Tacoma Morning News Tribune*

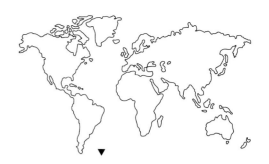

◀ **South Georgia Islands:** A young southern fur seal in a necklace of plastic fishnet. These mammals have been fighting for their lives for 100 years. By the end of the 19th century, populations of fur and elephant seals had been depleted by relentless hunting in polar seas. Their numbers have rebounded miraculously, yet the animals are not home free. Today, the threats they face are various and insidious: heavy metals, pesticides and PCBs. Marine scientists believe that plastic kills as many seals as oil spills. U.S. government biologists estimate that up to 50,000 northern fur seals are killed every year by entanglement in plastic fishnet fragments and other plastic debris. Mortality rates among the southern species of fur seal are anyone's guess. *Photo by: Frans Lanting/Minden Pictures*

◀ **Mar del Plata, Argentina:** Coastlines are among the most ecologically sensitive areas on earth. Yet during the summer months, people want to be by the ocean's side. In January and February, the height of the southern summer, the city of Buenos Aires adjourns to the beach. The population of Mar del Plata–normally 500,000–swells to more than three million, putting even more stress on the natural buffer between land and sea. *Photo by: Peter Lang/ Focus Stock Photo*

▲ **Westhampton, New York, USA:** A July storm assaults the Long Island coast. The ocean is territorial, jealous of its borders; yet we build right down to the high-tide mark. Our persistence in colonizing unsuitable habitats is remarkable. We build on beaches, flood plains, earthquake faults, volcanic rift zones, hillsides of tinder-dry chaparral. On being eroded, flooded, shaken or burned out, we build again. Shoreline development can be risky business, as these houses show. There are places on earth better left to nature. *Photo by: Mark Wexler/ Woodfin Camp & Assoc.*

▶ **Riachuelo River, Buenos Aires, Argentina:**
There are two sorts of black-water rivers in
Latin America. Some, like Brazil's Rio Negro,
are naturally dark from tannins produced by
decay in rainforest leaves. Others, like the
Riachuelo, are artificially blackened by toxins
dumped by tanneries and other industries.
The first sort are living rivers; the second sort
are dead.

Industrial growth along the Riachuelo has
been unplanned, and dumping goes unregu-
lated. A film of petroleum covers the river's
surface, blocking sunlight and the transpira-
tion of oxygen. To restore the river, specialists
believe, strict controls on sewage must be im-
posed, and, as in any intensive-care ward, oxygen provided. *Photo by: Diego Goldberg*

▲ **Hartford, Tennessee, USA:** The Pigeon River enters Hartford clean and emerges from the town as dark as chocolate. Since 1908, the local pulp mill has polluted the Pigeon with toxins. The river is famous now for its deformed carp and sludgeworms. Hartford has a nickname: "Widowville." These members of the Dead Pigeon River Council are holding photos of loved ones killed by cancer. *Photo by: Stephanie Maze/ National Geographic*

◄ **Köln, West Germany:** Sheep graze beneath factory stacks on the bank of the Rhine. The Rhine is one of the dirtiest rivers in Europe. About one-fifth of the world's production of chemicals occurs along its banks, yet twenty million Europeans depend on the Rhine for their drinking supply. *Photo by: Volker Hinz/Stern*

▶ **Le Puy, France:** The Loire is the longest river in France and the last wild river in Europe. A French environmental coalition, Loire Vivante, is determined to keep it that way. The group formed to fight construction of a series of dams that would shorten and tame the river. Here, on a December day, beneath the spires of the castle of Chabral, volunteers clean garbage from the Loire's banks and bottom. *Photo by: Bernard Hermann/Les Editions Didier Millet*

The dam is the ultimate symbol and most impressive artifact of humanity's attempt to improve on nature. "What is of all things most yielding/Can overcome that which is most strong?" the Chinese poet Lao Tzu asked 7,000 years ago. The answer is water. The dam is the engineer's attempt to controvert the poet's wisdom, to overcome the strength of water. Any dam is a complex mix of virtues and sins.

The Aswan dam project, in attempting to control the Nile and assure Egypt's future, drowned the Egyptian past, flooding temples, tombs and antiquities. By controlling annual flooding, it compromised the fertility of the Nile Valley, dependent since before the Pharoahs on nutrients deposited by those floods. By providing a habitat for the freshwater snails that spread schistosomiasis, it spawned debilitating epidemics.

In the southeastern Amazon, the Brazilian utility Electrobras is planning a dam on the Trombetas River that will clear more than 900 square kilometers of rainforest. The rising waters–a deluge universal to human myth–will be a surprise to several Indian tribes who have never had contact with outsiders; it will come as a shock as well to the other 35 communities flooded. Electrobras has not notified nearby residents about the project.

Electronorte, the company that built the Tucuruí and Balbina dams in the Amazon, proceeded more prudently, warning humans and evacuating a number of animals. But because of basic design problems, Balbina is a hydroelectric failure, providing only a trickle of the electricity projected. Though the World Bank at first denied funding for the dam because of its potentially severe environmental and social impact, it nonetheless covered the dam's completion costs. Owen Lammers of the International Rivers Network believes that international funding of such projects only worsens environmental degradation. "Until the World Bank makes policy changes," he says, "we're not going to see environmental improvements in the developing countries." *Photo essay by: Claus Meyer/Black Star*

◄ **Uatumã River, Brazil:** A hunter rescues a turtle endangered by the waters of the Uatumã rising behind Balbina Dam.

◀ **Tucuruí Dam, Tocantins River, Brazil:** The Tucuruí Dam, completed in 1985, has drowned more than 2,200 square kilometers of rainforest and displaced 5,000 families in four towns. It is expected to produce hydroelectric power for about 50 years before its reservoir becomes silted in.

▼ **Uatumã River, Brazil:** As the Uatumã's waters are stilled by construction of the Balbina Dam, trees drown on the reservoir's expanding shores. Two thousand square kilometers of rainforest ultimately will be flooded by the dam.

▶ **Balbina Reservoir, Brazil:** Two hundred hunters from the Tucuruí region, who became experts at animal rescue when their own land was flooded, were recruited to evacuate the creatures of the Uatumã in 1989. Every morning at seven o'clock, a flotilla of dozens of boats—small aluminum arks—searched the dying rainforest for refugee sloths, ant-eaters and primates as well as snakes, scorpions and armadillos. Here their boats unravel the labyrinth of the flooded forest, searching for dry land. On reaching it— a shrinking island, or the ever-receding main shore—they jump out with axes, lassos and nets. Of the 12,000 animals rescued at Balbina, 4,000 were sent to scientific institutions and the rest were released on high ground.

▲ **Budapest, Hungary:** János Vargha stands on a bank of the Danube, the river he has fought to save. In 1980, the governments of Hungary, Austria and Czechoslovakia planned a hydropower project that would dam the Danube in Czechoslovakia and divert it through a 16-kilometer canal to another dam in Hungary. The dams would flood forests, islands and the habitats of 200 protected plants and animals. Vargha's group, the Danube Circle, has succeeded–for now–in halting construction of the Hungarian dam. *Photo by: Peter Korniss*

◄ **Aral Sea, USSR:** The Aral Sea used to be the fourth-largest inland sea on earth. Then, in the 1960s, the Soviet Ministry of Water Resources embarked on a grand irrigation scheme to divert the rivers feeding the sea. Today the Aral Sea has lost 70 percent of its water. It used to yield 25,000 tons of fish annually; today the fish are gone. *Photo by: Richard Bangs/Sobek*

▶ **Mono Lake, California, USA:** Mono Lake, like all desert lakes, is a paradox: water in the desert, a wind-rippled expanse of coolness in the unrelenting heat. From a distance, the lake seems a mirage, an enormous improbability. Its blue is the only primary color in a basin of desert pastels. Its tufa formations–monuments and spires of calcium carbonate precipitated from underwater springs–add to the surreality. Drink from the lake and the illusion of oasis vanishes. Its waters are three times saltier than the sea and 80 times more alkaline.

The old dream of desert reclamation is another sort of mirage. The water for the dream must come from somewhere. To unmake one desert, engineers create a new one someplace else. The greening of the arid Los Angeles Basin has withered country all over the West. It has browned farms in Mexico and northern California, desertified the fertile ranchland of California's Owens Valley and reduced Owens Lake to an alkaline dustbowl. In Mono Lake, Owens Lake's surviving twin, decades of water diversion by Los Angeles is killing or dispossessing the ducks, gulls and shore birds of one of the most remarkable desert ecosystems known. Since 1941, Mono's level has dropped 41 feet; its shoreline is shrinking, its salts concentrating. Its rich and delicate ecosystem, dependent on brine shrimp and dominated by seabirds, has begun to fail.

The struggle for preservation of Mono Lake has been as bitter as any water war in the West, but there are signs of change. A citizens' group called the Mono Lake Committee and the Los Angeles Department of Water and Power, old enemies, are presently working together to find a solution that would protect the lake while meeting the city's water needs. *Photo by: Stephen Johnson*

◀ **Near Timbuktu, Mali:** More than 70 percent of the earth's surface is water, yet less than three percent of that water is fresh and an even smaller percentage clean. Where fresh water is scarce, carrying it is a principal job. In the drylands of developing countries, women and children spend hours of each day in that endeavor. *Photo by: Larry Price/Philadelphia Inquirer*

▲ **Kominde, Kenya:** Waterborne diseases in developing nations annually kill twenty-five million people, most of them children. The United Nations goal of providing clean water for everyone in the world by 1990 has not been met, in part as a result of its reliance on modern technology. When electric pump motors broke down, months passed before repairs could be made, and villagers often were forced to return to polluted sources. The U.N. is now encouraging the installation of hand-powered pumps, like the one built by these Kenyan women. *Photo by: Rainer Drexel/Bilderberg*

Matagalpa, Nicaragua: Coffee drying. *Photo by: Bill Gentile*

Himalayan foothills, Nepal: Rice terraces. *Photo by: Gordon Wiltsie*

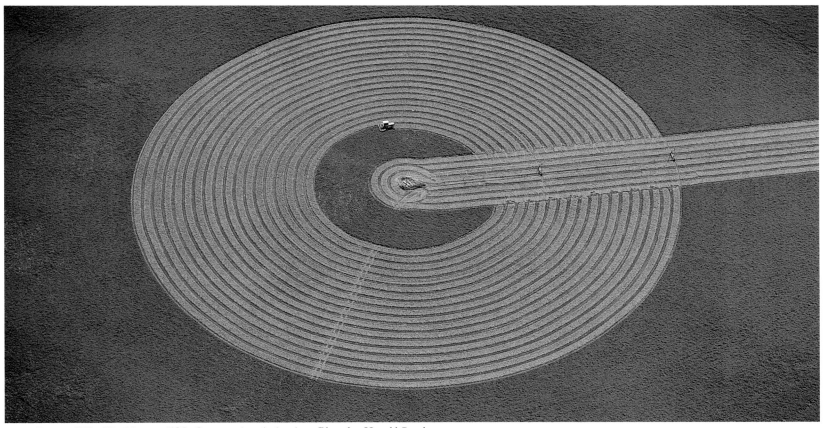

Horse Heaven Hills, Washington, USA: Center-pivot irrigation. *Photo by: Harald Sund*

Songpan, Sichuan, China: Family farm plots in central China. *Photo by: Yuan Xuejun*

◄ **Mt. Vernon, Ohio, USA:** Glenn and Rex Spray cultivate 700 acres of organic soy, corn, beans and hay in Knox County, Ohio. The Spray farm was one of 20 case studies chosen by the National Academy of Sciences in a recent report on alternative agriculture. The report concluded that American farms, if carefully managed and planted with diverse crops, can, with little or no application of chemicals, be as productive as–and more profitable than–farms dependent on pesticides and inorganic fertilizer. Indeed, during the drought of 1988, the Sprays had a more bountiful harvest than their neighbors. "We went organic 19 years ago, when we finally just started thinking for ourselves," says Glenn. "What we're doing is so simple," adds his brother, "that most farmers don't understand it." *Photo by: Randy Olson/ Pittsburgh Press*

▲ **Modesto, California, USA:** "What have they done to the rain?" asked a protest song of the 1960s. The concern then was rain carrying radioactive fallout. Acid rain was as yet unknown. "What have they done to the fog?" is the question of today. Research by the California Department of Food and Agriculture indicates that fog can transport pesticides used in orchards and vineyards to nearby vegetable farms, where they can taint the crops. Charlotte Schomburg, a soil scientist, checks a passive fog collector in the San Joaquin Valley, America's most fecund breadbasket. *Photo by: P.F. Bentley/Time*

◄ **Near Kuala Lumpur, Malaysia:** Pesticides banned in the U.S. are routinely exported to Third World countries. This Malay woman, spraying insecticide on a plantation of young palms, lacks even rudimentary protection from the poisonous mist. *Photo by: Paul Chesley*

49

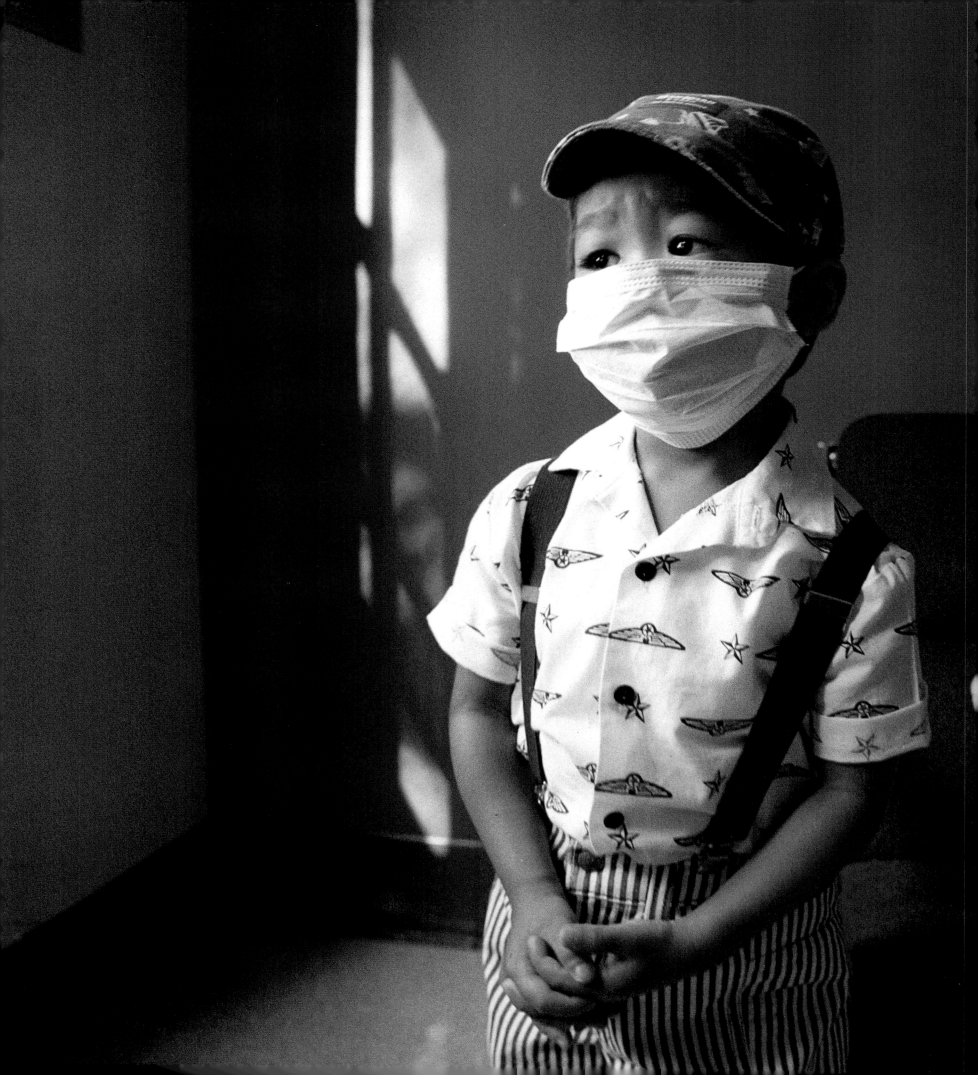

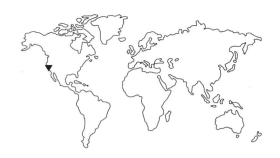

◀ **Bakersfield, California, USA:** On the American farm, pesticides are an addiction. Most are directed at insects, one of the most diverse and genetically malleable class of organisms on earth. Dusted with a new pesticide, many insects die, but survivors pass on resistent genes. One result of DDT use, aside from its decimation of the nation's songbirds, has been creation of supermosquitos that are impervious to DDT. The ingenuity of the pesticide manufacturers is no match for the mutability of the pests. With the invention of each new poisonous compound, the bugs re-invent themselves. For the farmer, it's a vicious cycle; for the pesticide manufacturer, a profitable one. Fields dependent on pesticides require heavier and heavier applications of newer and newer poisons. Rachel Carson's 1962 classic, *Silent Spring*, concentrated on the destruction of wildlife by pesticides. Today, concern has shifted to the human victims. "Cancer circles"–regions with abnormally high incidences of the disease–are multiplying in America's farmlands. A disproportionate number of the victims are children. In California's Central Valley, there are so many young cancer victims that Kern Medical Center has opened a special clinic for them. Richard Umali, three years old and suffering from leukemia, spends the afternoon in treatment. *Photo by: Rick Rickman*

◀ **León, Nicaragua:** One alternative to chemical pesticides is natural pest control. Here, a farm worker from the Intergrated Pest Management project in León sets out cones containing tiny *Trichogramma* wasps, natural enemies of the cotton bollworm. *Photo by: Lou Dematteis*

▶ **Biosphere II, Oracle, Arizona, USA:** Ladybugs are a natural insecticide, the only kind allowed in Biosphere II. An airtight, three-acre, glass-walled structure, Biosphere II contains the earth in microcosm: ocean, desert, savanna, tropical rainforest, saltwater marsh, freshwater marsh–and 3,800 species of plants and animals. Its designers hope Biosphere II will have space-station applications and offer opportunities for research in the ecology of closed systems. *Photo by: Peter Menzel*

◀ **Delano, California, USA:** As another alternative to pesticides, California strawberry growers have invented BugVac, a machine that generates just enough suction to remove lygus bugs from the tops of strawberry plants without disturbing the beneficial bugs that gather below. In Salinas, lettuce growers have developed Salad-Vac. Here, a third innovation, VAC-US, invented by Harold Nelson and Don Neumann of Delano, sucks leaf hoppers from grapevines. *Photo by: Rick Rickman*

◄ **Boston, Massachusetts, USA:** In the South
End-Lower Roxbury neighborhood of Boston,
more than 27,000 people live in an area of less
than a square mile. Any open space there is
accidental–most of it vacant lots cleared for
urban renewal in the 1960s. Residents have
turned many of these into vest-pocket parks,
urban gardens and mini-farms. The Trust
for Public Land is working with community
farmers and activists to protect these spaces.
Photo by: Susan Lapides

▲ **New York City, USA:** The South Bronx has
become a symbol of urban blight in the United
States. In the Hunts Point area, the Bronx
Frontier Development Organization has succeeded in bringing basic services, such as
sanitation and parks, back into a ravaged
neighborhood. The Hunts Point Farm, located
on three acres in the borough's old market
district, operates a greenhouse, a landscaping
business and a composting operation. Here,
Pedro Ramírez holds the beginnings of a
garden. *Photo by: Andy Levin*

◀ **Mali:** Through most of Africa, women are the farmers, producing 80 percent of the continent's food. Yet training programs and extension services are usually directed toward men. Lacking those resources, African women have organized farming cooperatives. In Tassakan, a cooperative on the banks of a small tributary of the Niger, a Mali woman harvests a tomato crop. *Photo by: Larry Price/Philadelphia Inquirer*

▲ **Balleyare, Niger:** The future of agriculture may lie in wisdom from the past. Modern petroleum-driven agri-business, in which vast acreages of a single crop–a monoculture–are treated with tons of chemicals, is not sustainable. Such agriculture mines the soil and poisons groundwater. Traditional farmers practice polyculture–growing many different crops on a given plot. They live close to the land, attentive to its natural fertility. Here, women of the Bella tribe, traditional agriculturalists, display their harvest. *Photo by: Ron Giling*

"The concept of the state, more-

over, is yielding rapidly at this

hour to the concept of the ecu-

mene, i.e., the whole inhabited

earth; and if nothing else unites

us, the ecological crisis will."

—Joseph Campbell

▶ **Mogadishu, Somalia:** Human progress is marked, we like to think, by a spread of knowledge. Our progress is marked just as surely by the spread of desert. The cradles of our civilization are dustbowls, our Edens withered. Man-made deserts occupy an area larger than Brazil. According to a survey by the United Nations Environment Program, 35 percent of the earth's land surface is in various stages of degradation to desert. The principal cause is the population explosion and humanity's forced expansion into ever drier and more marginal lands. With rain, poor fields and pastures will produce a few meager crops, a few head of sheep. With drought, the by-product will be desert. *Photo by: Michael Yamashita*

▲ **Mogadishu, Somalia:** The government of Somalia has mobilized volunteers and national rangeland employees to plant casuarina and cactus to stabilize encroaching dunes. *Photo by: Michael Yamashita*

◀ **Near Timbuktu, Mali:** Collecting firewood has been an important human endeavor since the invention of fire. Increased demand for fuel, however, has driven people to cut live trees, contributing heavily to land degradation. In Africa, a new type of cookstove is making a significant difference. Made from old drum cannisters, the stoves are built taller and narrower to produce more heat with less wood. *Photo by: Larry Price/Philadelphia Inquirer*

◀ **Madagascar:** (previous page) Dust and humanity: People walk to market through a parched sissal plantation. *Photo by: Frans Lanting/Minden Pictures*

▲ **Near Timbuktu, Mali:** In Africa, in the Americas, in Australia, Asia and Asia Minor, once-fertile lands are showing signs of desertification. At highest risk are the countries bordering the Sahara, where deforestation and overgrazing have, in some areas, all but destroyed the vegetation. Dust from that greatest of deserts blows across the Atlantic to pollute the skies of Florida. *Photo by: Larry Price/Philadelphia Inquirer*

▶ **Outside Timbuktu, Mali:** A boy stands by the Niger River. Mali lies in the Sahel, the great arid province just south of the Sahara. In the early 1970s, drought hit this semi-arid region, killing at least 100,000 people and millions of animals. The land faces continuing crises. *Photo by: Larry Price/Philadelphia Inquirer*

◄ **Korem, Ethiopia:** A family in a relief camp, victims of drought and famine, mourns the death of a child. About one hundred and thirty-five million people inhabit regions undergoing severe desertification. Of these, fifty million already have been seriously compromised in their ability to support themselves. The only practical way to prevent such degradation is to introduce better systems of land use: sustainable agriculture and conservation of natural resources. *Photo by: Mary Ellen Mark*

◀ **Osaka, Japan:** (previous page) Afternoon commuters cross the main intersection at Shibuya Station.

◀ In Japan's "capsule hotels," professionals with brief business in the city can pass a few hours or sleep overnight. These cozy sarcophagi are a peek, perhaps, at our own destiny. If the world population continues to grow at its current rate, by the year 2029 our present population of 5.3 billion will double. In 900 years there could be sixty million billion people– or 100 humans for every square yard of the earth's surface, land and sea. Physicist J.H. Fremlin has calculated that these 29th-century multitudes might be housed in a 2,000-story building covering the entire planet. The accommodations would look something like this. Fun for a night or two, maybe–but not for a lifetime. *Photos by: Paul Chesley*

▲ **Schiedam, Netherlands:** Habitations are crowded together in this most densely populated nation of Europe. "Elbow room!" cried Daniel Boone. He wouldn't have found it in Holland. *Photo by: Co Rentmeester/Image Bank*

▲ **Near Pekhu Tso, Tibet:** Three generations of a Dropka family live in this yak-hair tent. Called "the People of the Black Tents," Dropkas move their herds–and homes–with the seasons. The Dropka nomads "recycle" their yaks entirely: In the countryside where wood is nonexistent, yak dung fuels the family hearth; boots are made of yak leather, clothing of yak wool. The yak provides cheese, milk, meat and transportation. *Photo by: Galen Rowell/ Mountain Light*

▶ **Paramus, New Jersey, USA:** Shoppers at Toys R Us. Overconsumption is us. Americans use vastly more than their share of planetary resources. The average American consumes roughly 100 times the resources of one Munoru tribeswoman of Kenya and about 10 times as much as the average world citizen. Harvard zoologist E.O. Wilson has calculated that if the rest of the earth used raw materials at the rate the United States and Japan do, the planet could sustain a population of only 200 million. *Photo by: Nina Barnett*

◀ **Delhi, India:** International family planning organizations now cite a decent living standard, access to contraception and reduction of infant mortality rates as the most effective means to slow world population growth. Since many infants succumb to disease and malnutrition in poorer countries, couples have larger families to ensure that some children will reach adulthood–and provide "social security" to aging parents.

Women with more education and opportunities to earn income have healthier and fewer children. Here, women at a New Delhi clinic attend classes in literacy, female anatomy and contraceptive options. India became the first developing country to establish a national family planning program in 1951. During the 1970s, forced sterilization and other abuses created great suspicion about birth control programs. Voluntary family planning is now considered the only practical–and ethical–policy. Even with an ambitious voluntary family planning program, though, experts estimate that India's population, now 853 million, will exceed 1.4 billion by the year 2025. *Photo by: Judy Griesedieck*

▶ **Bondurant, Iowa, USA:** Family planning is not a concern unique to developing countries. At Bondurant-Farrar High School in suburban Des Moines, Steve Tucker and David Wallace learn about condoms. *Photo by: Dave Peterson/ Des Moines Register*

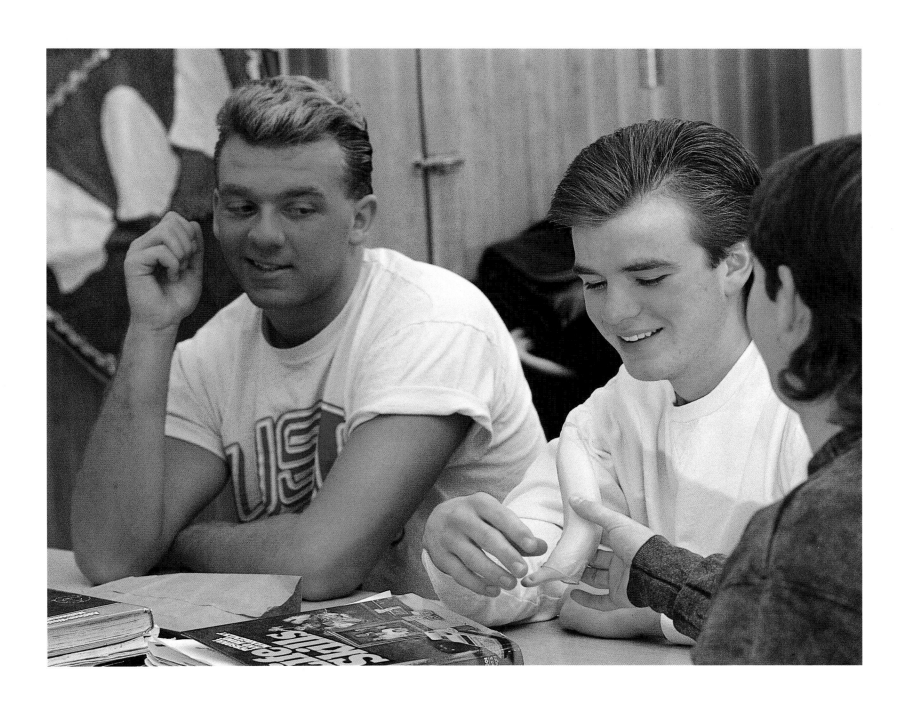

"For the first time in my life I saw

the horizon as a curved line. It

was accentuated by a thin seam of

dark blue light—our atmosphere.

Obviously, this was not the ocean

of air I had been told it was so

many times in my life. I was

terrified by its fragile appearance."

—Ulf Merbold, German astronaut

◀ **Kwajalein Atoll, Marshall Islands, Micronesia:** (previous page) In the low atolls of the Marshall Islands, the only real topography is in the sky. The upward temperature gradient is smooth, and huge cumulus clouds build to 50,000 feet and more. In the Marshallese language, the word *mejatoto* means "air, atmosphere, climate possessed by ghosts." The associations might seem a little superstitious, but they have proved curiously apt in the 20th century. In 66 nuclear blasts at Bikini and Enewetak atolls, the United States government contaminated hundreds of Marshall Islanders. Testing in the Marshalls ended with the Limited Test Ban Treaty of 1963. The ghosts of radiation have departed, and the clouds, once again immaculate, pile up to heaven. *Photo by: James Lerager*

◀ **Boston, Massachusetts, USA:** A Boston electricity plant spews smoke into the air. *Photo by: Ray Pfortner/Peter Arnold, Inc*

▲ **Belchen Mountain, Black Forest, Germany:** Half of all the trees in West Germany are dead or dying. A third of Swiss forests are sick or dead. Forests are moribund in much of Scandinavia and Eastern Europe, sick in France, Austria and the United Kingdom. The principal cause is believed to be acid rain. Heavy industry in Europe annually pumps an estimated fifty-five million tons of sulphur dioxide and thirty-seven million tons of nitrogen oxide into the air. The rain falls acidic and it falls anywhere, without regard for national boundaries. Poland's sulphur dioxide lands on Sweden; acid rain from America falls on Canadian soil. The problem is global, as its solution will have to be. *Photo by: Volker Hinz/Stern*

Los Angeles, California, USA: On a clear day, you can see L.A. *Photo by: Jim Mendenhall/Los Angeles Times*

Los Angeles, California, USA: Without any wind, it's smog city. *Photo by: Jim Mendenhall/Los Angeles Times*

▲ **Mexico City, Mexico:** Mexico City is the world's largest–and most polluted–city. Uncontrolled industrial wastes, combined with the emissions of three million automobiles, make the air a toxic soup. This bus actually may be part of the solution. In November, 1989, the government ordered drivers to leave their cars at home one day a week. *Photo by: Stephanie Maze/National Geographic*

▶ **Venice, Italy:** Bad air leaves us short of wind, then short of life. Eventually it defaces our very culture. Nowhere are the ravages of such pollution more startling than in Europe, where statues and monuments have been eaten away, leaving a grimy leprosy of stone. Venice, a repository of priceless artwork and architecture, is virtually under attack by air. An organization called Save Venice works to preserve its damaged monuments. Here, Antonio Leonardi cleans a statue. *Photo by: Raphaël Gaillarde*

◀ **Norbert, Quebec, Canada:** Acid rain has brought an artificial autumn to the sugar maples of Quebec. When the Quebec Resources Ministry began surveys of tree decline in 1983, about 29 percent of the province's maples had been affected. By 1986, the figure had jumped to 80 percent. Most of the acidity enters the atmosphere in sulphur dioxide emissions from U.S. factories. Unless those emissions are cut radically, one Canadian researcher warns, "maple syrup is just going to be a memory."

Acid rain is souring prospects for forests everywhere in the New World, as in the Old. Coniferous forests in the higher elevations of the Appalachians are dying, from Georgia to New England. Acid rain falling on southern Mexico and the Yucatan Peninsula is defacing the murals and megaliths of the Mayan Civilization.

As pollution poisons our lives, it also poisons our metaphors. Shakespeare once compared the quality of mercy to a "gentle rain from heaven." In Great Britain, the rain is no longer "gentle." One rainstorm that slapped Scotland had a pH of 2.4–as acidic as vinegar. Acid rain is one environmental problem we can easily do something about. Technology, such as "scrubbers" on factory stacks and catalytic converters on cars, can cut it substantially. All that is needed is the will to change things, as well as an investment of money.
Photo by: Sarah Leen

The Romanian dictator Nicolae Ceausescu built Copsa Mica as a "model" industrial city, and the town seems to have epitomized his regime. Ceausescu's Romania was equal parts dark Baltic fairytale and Orwellian prophecy–the labyrinth of secret tunnels under the capital city, the listening devices everywhere, the marble of the dictator's palace all the while shining white amidst the soot and poverty of his people.

Copsa Mica seems a town of chimneysweeps. The coal-fired smoke from its Karbosin plant is appalling, yet soot is the least of the town's worries. A nearby metallurgical factory generates an invisible pollution–unfiltered bioxide and mono-oxide of sulphur–that is far more lethal.

Copsa Mica's soil, milk and food are contaminated by lead and cadmium. The 6,000 townspeople suffer high rates of respiratory infection, anemia, premature birth, malnutrition, nervous disorders and retardation. Life expectancy is 55, and the retirement age is 50. Residents report that one in three babies is born dead.

Copsa Mica is a symbol, in fact, for all of Eastern Europe. In Poland, more than half of the water supply is too toxic even for industrial purposes. Polish air is the worst in Europe, and Poles with respiratory illness must flee underground. (Near Kraków there is a sanitarium in a salt mine 650 feet beneath the grime of the surface.) An East German automobile belches out 100 times more pollution than a West German car. East German forest is 41 percent dead or dying. In Czechoslovakia, 70 percent of the forest is damaged. "We have laid waste to our soils and the rivers and the forests that our forefathers bequeathed to us," playwright Vaclav Havel, transition president of Czechoslovakia, declared in his 1990 New Year's address.

There is an indomitability in the faces of Copsa Mica that is both a triumph and a little frightening. The human animal is almost *too* adaptable. We seem capable of accepting the most shocking degradation of our circumstances before we cry out. *Photo essay by: Tomas Muscionico/Contact Press Images*

◄ **Copsa Mica, Romania:** The Karbosin plant produces black carbon powder, and smoke darkens the life of the town.

Copsa Mica, Romania: Smudged ledgers in the personnel office at the Karbosin plant.

Copsa Mica, Romania: Women working inside the plant wear bandanas to try to protect themselves from the soot.

Copsa Mica, Romania: Almost all residents of the town are employed at the Karbosin plant. Here, one worker stands with his son.

Copsa Mica, Romania: The plant is so filthy that workers joke about "getting a breath of fresh air" by going outside for a cigarette.

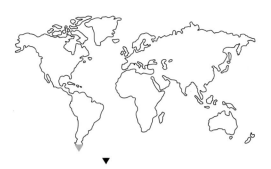

▶ **Antarctica:** No mainland is more remote from sources of pollution than Antarctica, but a steady rise in atmospheric carbon dioxide and other gases implicated in global warming has appeared even there. These gases let solar heat in but don't let it out, causing the "greenhouse effect." It was above remote Antarctica that the ozone hole was discovered. The hole forms each southern spring, growing larger nearly every year. Because the ozone layer screens out ultraviolet radiation, its disintegration has caused alarm. Here, the research ship *Polar Duke* studies the effect of increased ultraviolet radiation on marine organisms. *Photo by: Diego Goldberg*

▼ **Punta Arenas, Chile:** More than a century ago, Salesian priests established a meteorological observatory at Punta Arenas and recorded ground-level ozone readings. Today Punta Arenas lies under the ozone hole. This priest studies the old records. *Photo by: Diego Goldberg*

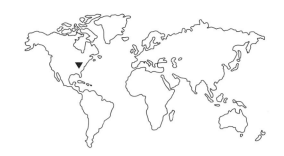

◀ **Kanawha River Valley, West Virginia, USA:**
Industry along this Ohio River tributary is almost exclusively chemical factories. The narrow river valley and its frequent fog-inversion layer trap chemical waste in the air and water, making the area one of the most polluted in the country. Its nickname: "Cancer Valley."
Photo by: Wally McNamee/Newsweek

▼ **Institute, West Virginia, USA:** Lois Gibbs addresses a rally outside a plant in "Cancer Valley." Gibbs, a former Niagara Falls resident, was among the first to sound the alarm about Love Canal, America's best-known toxic dump disaster. After two years of protests, Gibbs and her neighbors held two EPA officers hostage. Love Canal was eventually declared a Federal Disaster Area. Gibbs moved to Arlington, Virginia, where she founded the Citizens Clearinghouse for Hazardous Wastes.
Photo by: Wally McNamee/Newsweek

▶ **Bhopal, India:** Between 1980 and 1984, there were six accidents at Union Carbide's pesticide plant in Bhopal. Then, on December 2, 1984, 30 tons of methyl isocyanate gas escaped in an accident that experts believe resulted from poor management and faulty equipment. The poisonous cloud killed at least 2,500 people and permanently injured thousands. Bhopal's survivors suffer a myriad of disabilities, including lung damage, reproductive problems, abdominal pain, lassitude, conjunctivitis and blindness. *Photo by: Pablo Bartholomew/Gamma Liaison*

▲ **Dorchester, Massachusetts, USA:** Manuela Teixeira watches Peter Maiuri, a worker from Boston's Lead Free Kids project, remove toxic soil from her yard. Frozen ground makes the jackhammer necessary; the problem Maiuri is attacking is obdurate in more ways than one. At least three million American pre-schoolers have harmful levels of lead in their blood.

Homes built before the 1950s were covered inside and out with lead paint. The lead, inhaled as dust or eaten as chips, can cause attention disorders and learning disabilities. Lead poisoning is gravest in Northeastern and Midwestern cities, particularly among the urban poor, most of whom live in older housing. Manuela, eight years old, has tested positive for lead contamination. *Photo by: Bill Greene/ Boston Globe*

▶ **Seymour, Indiana, USA:** A worker draws a sample from a drum of hazardous waste to determine the nature of its toxins. Generating poisonous by-products is vastly easier than disposing of them. In the first eight years of the federal Superfund program, only 34 of the 1,175 worst sites were cleaned. *Photo by: Kevin Horan/Picture Group*

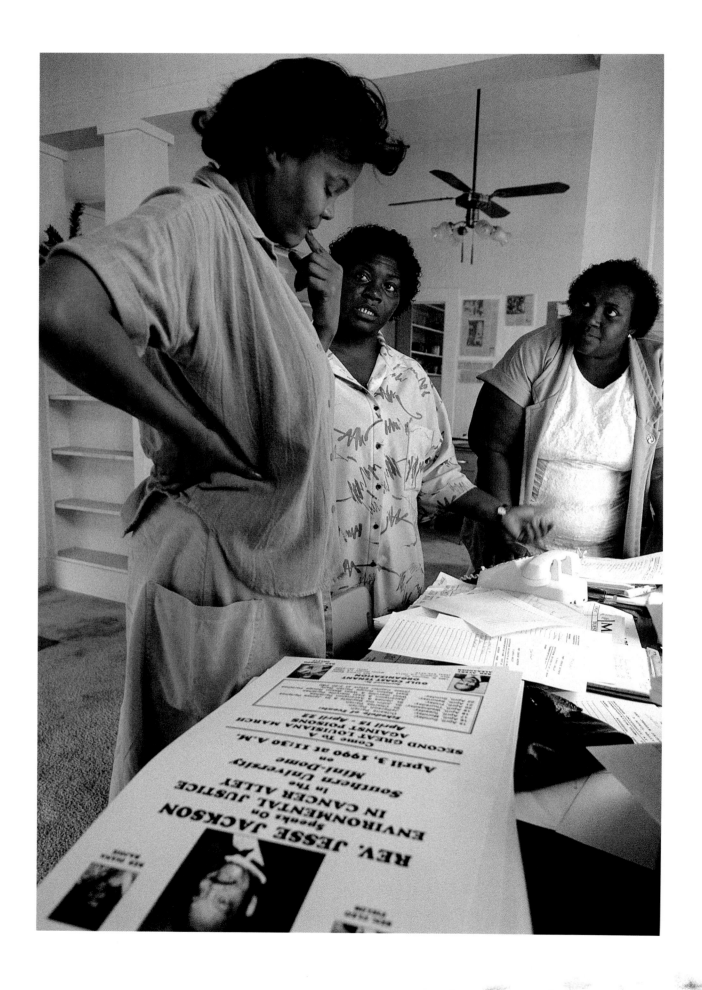

◄ **Baton Rouge, Lousiana, USA:** One-fifth of U.S. petrochemicals are produced on the banks of the Mississippi between Baton Rouge and New Orleans–a stretch known as the "Petro-chemical Corridor." Along the corridor every year, tons of carcinogenic and mutagenic compounds leak into the groundwater or are pumped into the river. Louisiana has the third-worst air and the second-worst water in the nation. Residents of one corridor town, accustomed to fleeing their homes after spills, were warned that going outside could kill them. A local company suggested that people try an alternate defense, called "buttoning up": shutting off air-conditioners, chinking door cracks with blankets and putting wet cloths over their faces. Here, three inhabitants of Monte Sano Village –Mildred Jean Henderson, Betty Ewing and Sharon Lewis–prepare for a march against toxics. *Photo by: Nicole Bengiveno/New York Daily News*

▲ **Petrochemical Corridor, Louisiana, USA:** In the 1988 Great Louisiana Toxics March, a new environmental alliance of black and white residents protested chemical dumping in their communities by joining in a march that traversed the entire 85 miles from Baton Rouge to New Orleans. *Photo by: Sam Kittner*

▲ **Los Angeles, California, USA:** MELA, Mothers of East Los Angeles, and CCSCLA, the Concerned Citizens of South-Central Los Angeles, demonstrate against the proposed $29 million Vernon incinerator, which would burn 125,000 pounds of toxic waste a day less than four miles from downtown L.A. Typically, the site is not in an affluent community but in a poor town. A 1987 study found that more than 40 percent of the nation's blacks, and half of its Hispanics, live in communities with at least one uncontrolled toxic-waste site. For the time being, MELA has halted construction of the incinerator through court appeals. *Photo by: Rick Rickman*

◄ **Nitro, West Virginia, USA:** Businesses and schools stand within several hundred yards of this abandoned chemical-processing plant. Taxpayers will foot the $12-million bill to clean it up. *Photo by: Sam Kittner*

▶ **Malville, France:** Two eras meet at Malville, 50 kilometers southwest of Lake Geneva, where steam from the stacks of the Super-Phoenix Reactor rises above an old stone church. France, which has 55 nuclear reactors on line, relies more heavily on nuclear power than any other nation.

In the 1970s, virulent public opposition to the Malville Super-Phoenix–a superbreeder that stores large amounts of plutonium, the most toxic substance known–swept the French countryside. In June of 1979, police fired tear gas and concussion grenades at students, peasants, families and factory workers protesting at Malville. Many were wounded, and a 31-year-old man, Vital Michalon, was killed. Nonetheless, the Super-Phoenix went on line.

For the past decade, the French government's heavy financial investment in nuclear power and its successful publicity campaign have quelled the controversy. Indeed, France is fast becoming the nuclear clearinghouse of Western Europe: England made plans to import nuclear-generated power from France after British protests halted some of the country's atomic-energy production. Germany is considering exporting its nuclear waste to be reprocessed in France. Still, the French nuclear industry faces the same problems afflicting nuclear power production everywhere: waste disposal, reactor down-time, vulnerability to sabotage, escalating uranium costs–and the possibility of an accident. *Photo by: Bernard Hermann/Les Editions Didier Millet*

▶ **Chernobyl, Ukraine, USSR:** Family members hold a wake for Anna Mikhailovna, a resident of Chernobyl's "Dead Zone." In April, 1986, an explosion and fire at the Chernobyl Atomic Power Station caused a meltdown of the reactor core and sent at least seven tons of radioactive material into the atmosphere. Food and water through much of Europe were contaminated. The Dead Zone, an uninhabitable area of 2,600 square kilometers, was declared around the ruined plant, and 135,000 Ukrainians were evacuated.

Twenty-eight people died within 75 days from acute radiation poisoning. They were only the beginning. The nature of radiation injury, and of the latency period for cancer, is such that casualties in the Ukraine, as well as the rest of Europe, will continue to mount through most of the next century. The U.S. Department of Energy estimates that cancers induced by the accident will kill 39,000 people. Physicist John Gofman has put the number at one million. One irony–as victims of American nuclear testing and nuclear accidents have discovered– is that none of these thousands will be able to "prove" that he or she is a victim. No cancer can be traced with absolute certainty to its origin. When Anna Mikhailovna died of a lung ailment in December, 1989, three years after the accident, her family was convinced–even if health researchers were not–that the cause lay in the melted reactor at Chernobyl. *Photo by: Charles Fox/Philadelphia Inquirer/Matrix*

◄ **Fuchu, Japan:** The nuclear age brought with it a new language. The most poignant of its terms are those for the victims. "Kobaam ke?" Marshall Islanders ask: "Were you bombed? Are you a victim of radioactive fall-out?" When the United States tested the hydrogen bomb in the Marshall Islands, it destroyed the atoll of Bikini and dispossessed its inhabitants. When the wind blew the wrong way, the people of Rongelap and Utirik atolls were poisoned.

The Marshallese word for the irradiated folk is *rubaam*, "people of the bomb." The Japanese synonym is *hibakusha*. Busuke Shimoe, now 86 years old, is one of the latter. Here he holds the jacket he wore in Hiroshima on August 6, 1945, when the atomic bomb exploded less than a mile away. The fingers of his right hand melted and fused. His wife and daughter were among the 210,000 killed. Today Shimoe has cancer–and so does his son. *Photo by: Karen Kasmauski*

107

The *rubaam* and *hibakusha* of the United States are called "downwinders." Some downwinders are military personnel exposed to nuclear fallout during Pacific tests. Many more are residents of Nevada, where nuclear testing started in the early 1950s. During four decades of testing by the U.S. and Britain, the desert has been rocked by more than 900 atomic blasts. An estimated 25,000 desert dwellers in three states–and two million citizens nationwide–were exposed to high levels of radiation. Public alarm about its health effects led to the signing of the 1963 Limited Test Ban Treaty, which forced nuclear testing underground, making a moonscape of the Nevada desert (below, left).

The same kind of tests have taken place for more than 40 years in the Soviet Republic of Kazakhstan. In February, 1989, radioactive gases escaped from underground nuclear tests. Renowned Kazakh poet Olzhas Suleimenov, appearing on television to recite verse, read instead a statement against nuclear testing and called for a mass meeting. Five thousand people arrived and gave birth to the Nevada-Semipalatinsk Movement, so named to emphasize kinship with the American movement against nuclear testing. Pressure from the Nevada-Semipalatinsk Movement cut the number of Soviet underground tests in 1989 by more than half. The Intermediate-range Nuclear Forces (INF) Treaty, signed by presidents Gorbachev and Reagan in December, 1987, took a first step toward reducing nuclear stockpiles, if only by 3 percent. Destruction of the missiles (below, center) is certified by teams of Soviet and American inspectors charged with verifying compliance by both sides (below, right).

▶ **Mercury, Nevada, USA:** Demonstrators at the test site. *Photo by: Andy Levin*

Photo by: Karen Kasmauski

Photo by: Yuri Kuidin

Photo by: Yuri Kuidin

YOU ARE NOW ENTERING
NEVADA TEST SITE
NO TRESPASSING
BY ORDER OF THE UNITED STATES
DEPARTMENT OF ENERGY

◄ **Wackersdorf, Bavaria, West Germany:** German anti-nuclear activists pray, as is their custom every Sunday at two o'clock, at the site of their greatest triumph. In 1985, the Bonn government began construction of a nuclear reprocessing plant in Wackersdorf. By the end of the 1980s, Wackersdorf had become the main focus of the German anti-nuclear movement. Clashes between the police and an alliance of local villagers and other nuclear opponents were the most violent of the decade. But it was not until construction costs multiplied that the project was cancelled. The plant at Wackersdorf is to be converted to solar and other "soft" technologies. *Photo by: Volker Hinz/Stern*

"*The forest is a peculiar organism of unlimited kindness and benevolence that makes no demands for its sustenance and extends generously the products of its life and activity; it affords protection to all beings...*" —*Gautama Buddha*

The tropical rainforest is the richest ecosystem on earth, with the tropical reef a close second. "If the traveller notices a particular species," scientist Sir Alfred Russel Wallace wrote of the Malaysian rainforest, "and wishes to find more like it, he may often turn his eyes in vain in every direction. Trees of varied forms, dimensions and colours are all around him, but he rarely sees any of them repeated." For a visitor whose forests have been temperate, the variety is bewildering. In the coniferous forest of the North American West, the traveler often finds himself in vast stands of a single species–lodgepole pine or redwood or ponderosa. In the mixed-deciduous forests of the Northeast, he finds himself in woodland where five or six species predominate. In the South American or Malaysian or African jungle, he is lost amid hundreds of species growing on a given acre.

What is true for trees is true for animals. We have only begun to catalogue and name the creatures of the rainforest. The rainforest canopy, where most jungle life goes on, remains terra incognita. Biology classes of the 1960s taught that as many as one million species of insect might exist on earth. In the early 1970s, Terry Erwin of the Smithsonian Institution developed a technique for fogging the canopy with insecticide, then counting what dropped to the ground. In the Panamanian rainforest, from 19 specimens of a single tree species, he collected 1,200 species of beetle alone. He has estimated that there are from ten to thirty million insect species in the canopy.

What is true for trees and animals is also true for people. Humanity has diversified in the rainforest. The Yanomami, the largest group of unacculturated Indians in Brazil, speak a language unrelated to any other spoken in the Amazon Basin or anywhere else on earth. They have a world-view of their own, and their forest is full of treasures.

◀ **Rio Branco, Brazil:** (previous page) *Photo by: Claus Meyer*

▶ **Roraima, Brazil:** Yanomami Indians in a forest clearing. *Photo by: Claus Meyer*

▲ **Jari River, Brazil:** Ranchers, farmers, loggers, miners and homesteaders have all carved out pieces of the Amazon. Brazil has the most tropical forest in the world. It is also experiencing the worst losses: between twelve million and twenty-two million acres a year, according to the World Resources Institute. Here, a worker uses his chainsaw to cut rainforest at the edge of the Jari Project. This gargantuan wood pulp and livestock operation, the size of Connecticut, was a dream of the American shipping magnate Daniel Ludwig, who founded it in 1967. Like most grandiose reworkings of nature, it was an ecological catastrophe. Ludwig departed in 1982, and ownership of the plantation reverted to Brazil. *Photo by: Kevin Horan/ Picture Group*

▶ **Rondonia, Brazil:** In 1987, 80,600 square kilometers of rainforest, an area one-fifth the size of California, went up in smoke. The fires were deliberate: the simplest way for cattle ranchers and homesteaders to clear new land. The repercussions were global: as the rainforest gets smaller, it absorbs less carbon dioxide, contributing to the warming trend. The burning forest adds even more carbon dioxide to the atmosphere. *Photo by: Stephen Ferry/JB Pictures*

▲ **Agriguemes, Rondonia, Brazil:** Humped Zebu cattle graze on the Nova Vida ranch, 62,000 acres carved from Amazonian wilderness. Such spreads are all hardscrabble ranches. A paradox of rainforest lushness is that the soils supporting it are poor. The jungle is an efficient recycler: All the nutrients are absorbed by the trees, with little left in the soil. The "new life" of the Nova Vida ranch is certain to be brief. *Photo by: J. Kyle Keener/Philadelphia Inquirer/Matrix*

◄ **Brazil:** Dirt road and charred forest in Amazonia. In the late 1960s, the Brazilian government sponsored a program to build roads into the heart of the rainforest for settlers and industry. The road is often the beginning of the end for any wilderness. The southern state of Rondonia has lost 30 percent of its forest. If development continues at the present pace, the forest will be almost gone in 10 years. *Photo by: H.W. Silvester/Rapho/Black Star*

◄ **Roraima, Brazil**: Intravenous tubes and Yanomami hammocks. In the past two years, 45,000
prospectors have invaded Yanomami lands
looking for gold. In October, 1989, then-Presi-
dent José Sarney ordered the miners out. The
miners threatened guerrilla war and Sarney
reversed himself, allowing them to stay and
reducing by decree the Yanomami homeland
from 36,000 to 800 square miles. When the in-
vasion of the miners began, there were about
9,000 Yanomami. Today, they are dying in
large numbers from tuberculosis, hepatitis, ma-
laria and venereal diseases. *Photo by: Claus Meyer*

▲ **Rondonia, Brazil**: The 23 square kilometers
of the Alto Paraiso tin mine were cleared from
the Amazon forest. Two years ago, the "high
paradise" of the mine was a real paradise, an
Eden of pristine rainforest. For the next millen-
nium or two, it will be desert. *Photo by: J. Kyle
Keener/Philadelphia Inquirer/Matrix*

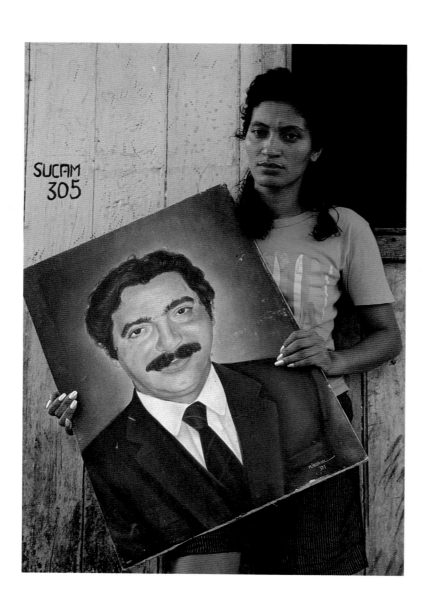

◄ **Xapuri, Brazil:** Ilzamar Mendes holds a portrait of Chico Mendes, her assassinated husband. Chico Mendes Filho was a poor man who earned his living as a rubber tapper. Since the turn of the century, rubber tappers have extracted latex from the trunks of rubber trees in the Amazon, earning subsistence wages. Mendes set about to better their plight. In 1985, he organized the National Council of Rubber Tappers, a union 30,000-strong that created cooperatives and forest alliances throughout the Amazon. The goal was to improve the lot of the tappers and to preserve the rainforest from which they extracted their living.

The tappers encountered bitter conflict from cattle ranchers and other large landowners, who wanted to continue cutting down the forest. Mendes, who survived five attempts on his life by hired assassins, was shot to death on December 22, 1988. His work lives on in the continuing determination of the tappers and in 12 rubber-tree reserves, totaling more than five million acres, that are being created in the Amazon. Mendes is now an international symbol of environmental courage–and of hope for the forests of Amazonia. *Photo by: Mark Edwards*

▶ **Rio Branco, Brazil:** Thousands of Brazilians marched in the fall of 1989 to support preservation of the rainforest. *Photo by: Gustavo Gilabert/ JB Pictures*

▲ **Sarawak, Malaysia:** The tropical rainforest of Sarawak in Borneo is being logged as rapidly as any on earth. The forest's native people—the Penan, Iban, Kayan, Pelabit and others—are being dispossessed, and their cultures annihilated. In the past few years, more than 100 Penan and Iban tribespeople, supported by Friends of the Earth Malaysia, have been arrested for setting up roadblocks in an attempt to stop the logging trucks. *Photo by: Paul Chesley*

▶ **Dhaka, Bangladesh:** Plague, flood, famine, pestilence: The history of Bangladesh is a recitation of catastrophe. No land better illustrates how nature's calamities can be exacerbated by the works of human beings. Deforestation in the Himalayas by mountain peoples has heightened monsoon flooding in the Bengal Delta. In the 1988 floods shown here, 1,200 Bangladeshis died and twenty-five million were left homeless. Deforestation at the other extreme of elevation,

a sea-level clearing of mangrove forest for rice paddies by the Bangladeshis themselves, destroyed a natural barrier to the sea. When a tidal wave hit the unprotected coast in 1970, at least 300,000 people died. Since then, Bangladesh has begun mending its sea fences with a large-scale mangrove replanting project. *Photo by: Chip Hires/Gamma Liaison*

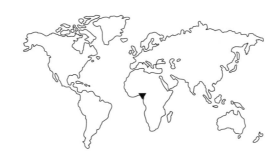

"Wilderness," Nancy Newhall wrote in *This Is the American Earth*, "holds answers to more questions than we know how to ask." No wilderness holds more answers to unarticulated questions than the tropical rainforest. To those few questions we have succeeded in formulating, the rainforest's answers have been electrifying. Vincristine, a drug made from the leaves of the rosy periwinkle–a rainforest plant –offers the victims of lymphocytic leukemia a 99 percent chance of remission. Cortisone, used to treat rheumatoid arthritis, was originally derived from wild tropical yams. So was Diosgenin, the active ingredient in birth-control pills. There are dozens of others. We can only begin to guess how many more await us in the jungle. Fewer than one percent of tropical forest species have been analyzed for their chemical properties. The tropical forest is the deepest gene pool on earth, the widest reservoir of species diversity. Farmers in search of insects as biological controls for pests, crop breeders looking for genes with which to fortify new strains of food plants, have no better place to look than the rainforest.

According to the U.S. National Academy of Sciences, fifty million acres of tropical forest–an area the size of England, Scotland and Wales combined–is lost or degraded every year. Early in human history, tropical forest covered 12 percent of the planet's land surface. Now it covers only eight percent. The Penan people of Borneo are fighting for their rainforests. The Kayapo of Brazil are fighting for theirs. The Philippines have banned all logging exports. Dr. José Luzenberger, Brazil's most clarion voice for the Amazon rainforest, has been appointed Interior Minister of his country. We must save what's left of the rainforest, pause for a breath–and then begin dreaming up all those questions as yet unasked of it.

▶ **Yaounde, Cameroon:** A scientist tests plant extractions for medicinal value. *Photo by: George Steinmetz*

Rainforest lichen. *Photo by: John Werner*

Tamerin lion monkey. *Photo by: Claus Meyer*

Plumeria blossom. *Photo by: John Werner*

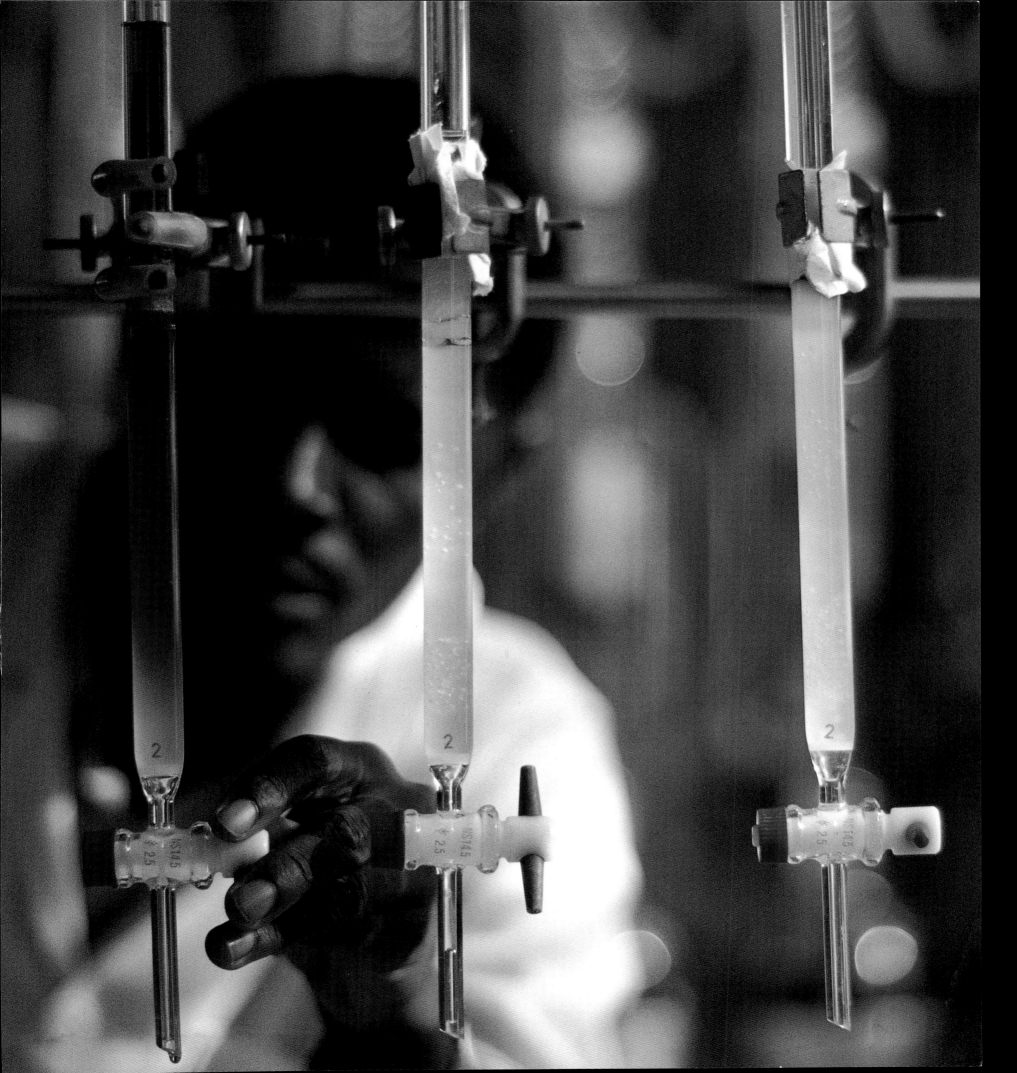

◄ **Mt. Hood National Forest, Oregon, USA:**
(previous page) Old-growth forest along the
Salmon River. This is the forest primeval,
where nature still rules by its own laws. The
Douglas firs grow for hundreds of years, then
fall according to their own schedules. *Photo by:
George Wuerthner*

◄ **Washington, USA:** Few languages are more
mendacious than the language of the timber industry. The great trees of the Northwestern forest are home, in life, to spotted owls, marbled
murrelets, squirrels, fishers and bears. In death,
they become seed logs to new generations of
saplings. To the timber industry, however, they
are "overmature," a burden on the forest. They
need cutting down. The most economical way
to do that is in a "clear-cut." The effects are
devastating. A clear-cut exposes an entire hill-
side to the full impact of sun and wind, disrupt-
ing vital ecological links and damaging long-

term productivity. In the mid-1800s, there were
twenty million acres of old-growth forest in Oregon and Washington. Only two to three million
acres remain today. If the area had been logged
selectively, a new forest would now be growing.
Photo by: Daniel Dancer

▲ **Fort Bragg, California, USA:** This mill, operated
by Georgia Pacific–one of the largest lumber
companies in the country–is among those that
are cutting the giant conifers of the Northwest.
Photo by: Reg Morrison/Weldon Owen

◄ **Quinalt Indian Reservation, Washington, USA:**
One virtue of the clear-cut, we're told by the timber industry, is that it clears the way for a "tree farm." The tree farm is largely illusion; its greatest virtues are cosmetic. When planted in strips along roads, tree farms hide the logging scars behind them. The timber industry talks a great deal about how many trees it replants in farms, but it says little about how many of those trees survive. Forests reproduce themselves much better on their own. They cannot be farmed for long. The soil profile declines precipitously with each cut. Two crops are possible, sometimes three, then the soil is finished.

In the U.S. we work overtime to log our last old-growth forests, even as we chide Brazilians about their destruction of their own. We fault Brazil for its treatment of Amazonian Indians, forgetting the bleak history of our treatment of Indians here. The U.S. Bureau of Indian Affairs has done poorly by the forests of the Quinalt Reservation on Washington's Olympic Peninsula. When the land was leased to timber companies, bureau regulations did not require removal of logging debris or subsequent re-planting. Today, the Quinalt forests are a wasteland that the tribe's forestry program is working to revive. Here two Quinalts, Joseph Sanchez and James Bastian, plant new trees.
Photo by: Jim Richardson

133

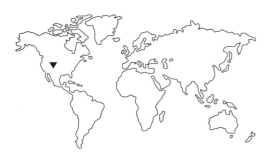

▶ Yellowstone National Park, Wyoming, USA:
Fireweed flowers amidst the burnt trees of the
great Yellowstone fires. The raging fires of
1988 burned 793,880 acres of Yellowstone Park.
On August 20, "Black Saturday," the blaze grew
in size by about 160,000 acres. The Park Service
was much maligned for its fire-management
policies, but the fires were largely natural, part
of a 200- or 300-year cycle that had last blackened Yellowstone in 1700.

The Yellowstone ecosystem was prepared. The
heat of the fire melted the resin sealing the
cones of lodgepole pines. The cones popped
open, and from between the scales dropped
seeds that for decades had been awaiting the
flames. They fell on open, sun-lit, charred land
of precisely the sort that lodgepole seedlings
prefer for their germination. The lodgepole is
the phoenix of pines, a tree designed to burn
and then reproduce itself. The aspen, another
fire-tolerant species, resprouted from its own
underground roots. Fireweed quickly took over
the burned-over understory.

Yellowstone's large animals–elk, bear and
bison–ran out of the fire's path, then returned
to their old haunts when things cooled off. Insects returned quickly, reclaiming trees killed
and scorched by the flames. Field mice and
chipmunks came on the heels of the insects.
Woodpeckers flew in to profit from the bark
beetles and other insects that were feeding off
the dead snags. Tree swallows, sapsuckers and
flickers built nests in the cavities hollowed out
by woodpeckers. Today Yellowstone is green
again, once more beginning its periodic renais-
sance from ashes.

The lesson in fireweed is that nature can
handle natural calamities. Given a chance–not
too many calamities in succession–the earth
bounces back. *Photo by: Renee Lynn*

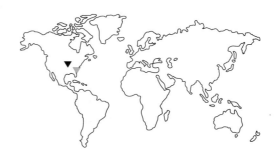

▲ **Kansas City, Missouri, USA:** On All Species
Day in Kansas City in May, 1989, a "phantom
forest" sprouted in Volker Park. Volunteers
planted 1,800 five-foot-high stacks of newspapers. Each stack represented a 40-foot pine; the
total equaled the quantity of pulpwood cut for
one printing of the city's Sunday paper. The
phantom forest demonstrated a number of
things: That no news is good news for the forest. That one should not miss the forest for
the headlines and the sports. That recycling is
important. *Photo by: Steven Pierce*

◄ **Atlanta, Georgia, USA:** Mountains of newsprint are sorted at the Southeast Recycling
Corporation. In 1988, 13.7 million tons of
newsprint were produced in the U.S.–about
120 pounds per person. A third of that newsprint is now recycled. *Photo by: Stephanie Maze/
National Geographic*

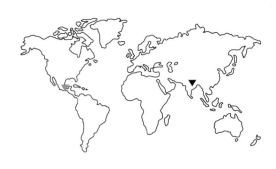

◄ **Mt. Everest, Nepal:** Today, garbage piles up to the top of the world. After a half-century of expeditions, Everest Base Camp is a dump, the old oxygen bottles and trash of a thousand climbs preserved by ice and cold air. *Photo by: Seny Norasingh*

► **Netzahualcoyotl slum, Mexico City, Mexico:** Overpopulation meets recycling. Low wages in the Mexican countryside have prompted an exodus of Mexican peasants to their capital city, the greatest megalopolis on earth. The result is that many hundreds of thousands end up living on the outskirts in squatters' barrios like this one. Inhabitants of the Netzahualcoyotl dump live in tents of plastic and cloth, or in makeshift houses of cardboard, barrels and tires. They collect recyclable materials and sell them for a few pesos. The lucky ones are admitted to the Union of Garbage Pickers, an exclusive organization that strictly monitors its territory. Here two young *pepenadores* (scavengers), Juan and Javier, warm themselves by a fire after a hard day's picking. *Photo by: Ricardo DeAratanha/ Los Angeles Times*

▲ **New York Harbor, USA:** In the summer of 1988, medical waste–bandages, syringes, vials of blood–began washing up on Long Island's shores. Suddenly, people seemed to wake to how badly the oceans are being trashed. If the old symbol for our excesses on the sea is *Pequod*, Ahab's legendary whaleship, then the new one is this garbage scow from Islip. Forbidden to dump at sea, the barge traveled up and down the Eastern seaboard but found no landfill that would accept its load. Here it sits in New York Harbor, with 3,100 tons of Long Island trash and no port to call home. After five months, the garbage was finally unloaded and burned in a New York incinerator. *Photo by: Dennis Capolongo*

◀ **Staten Island, New York, USA:** New York City generates 30,000 tons of waste a day. Much of it ends up in Fresh Kills Landfill, the largest garbage dump on earth. *Photo by: Nina Barnett*

▲ **West Milford Township, New Jersey, USA:**
Tanja Vogt may one day be known as the leader of the Jersey Styrofoam Rebellion. Vogt learned that the manufacturing of polystyrene, commonly known by the brand name Styrofoam, releases chlorofluorocarbons that destroy atmospheric ozone. After a brief, shining moment of usefulness–seldom longer than the time it takes coffee to cool–polystyrene suffers a long-lingering death. It clutters our landscapes and overtaxes our landfills. When Vogt discovered that recyclable trays would cost only five cents more than the polystyrene trays her school had been using, 80 percent of her classmates volunteered the extra nickel. Polystyrene trays were banned in West Milford Township schools, then in other schools throughout New Jersey. *Photo by: Ed Keating*

▶ **New York City, USA:** Nine states have now passed bottle and can recycling bills, requiring beverage manufacturers to make containers returnable and reuseable. Congress is considering a proposal that would mandate such recycling nationwide. In New York City, a program run by the homeless called WE CAN helps the environment by redeeming mountains of cans and bottles collected from the streets. *Photo by: Andy Levin*

◄ **Machida, Japan:** A Japanese technician, a new sort of Midas, displays his waste pellets. It is no coincidence that Japan, a country with few natural resources, is at the forefront of waste management. In the city of Machida, garbage disposal is an art. The city's $65-million "recycling culture center" opened in 1982. Today it collects about 100,000 tons of garbage a year, recycling 90 percent of it. Trash is turned into pellets, rotting food becomes fertilizer and discarded household appliances are renovated for reuse. *Photo by: Torin Boyd*

▲ **Toyota City, Japan:** The Katsu Ichikawa Company annually collects 1,700 tons of discarded computers from all over Japan. The company recycles such components as silicon chips, monitors and parts of circuit boards. *Photo by: Torin Boyd*

► **Nishi Rokugo, Japan:** (following page) The Tire Koen–"Tire Park"–of the Tokyo suburb of Nishi Rokugo has recycled thousands of old tires. Most tires end up rotting in landfills, but here there are tire swings and slides and bridges, tire robots, tire rockets and tire pyramids. This Godzilla of tires is a monster reformed. Instead of destroying Tokyo–the creature's old habit–it is helping to clean up the city. *Photo by: Torin Boyd*

"As a people we have developed

a life-style that is draining

the earth of its priceless and

irreplaceable resources without

regard for the future of our

children and people all around

the world." — Margaret Mead

149

▶ **Ludwigshafen, West Germany:** The Rhine River flows through one of the most industrialized–and polluted–areas of Europe. After World War II, when West Germany began to rebuild, cities based on heavy industry sprouted around the nation's mining areas. *Photo by: Volker Hinz/Stern*

◀ **Kilauea Volcano, Hawaii, USA:** (previous page) When Kilauea erupts at night, the sky turns red over the southern end of the Big Island of Hawaii. It is eerie and unnatural, as if the sun, just gone down, has changed its mind and decided to rise again. It's a scene from some eon early in the earth's formation. It is the strangest sensation to drive in two lanes of 20th-century traffic toward that Pre-Cambrian sky.

Rounding a turn, one sees the fountain of lava itself, a thousand-foot, incandescent bright orange pillar against a red heaven. The roar is like a jet engine in perpetual take-off. Now and again the fountain rockets higher, spinning off a graceful, wraith-like flare of illuminated smoke. One understands suddenly why Pele, goddess of volcanoes, is the Hawaiian divinity that remains most alive for modern Hawaiians. From time to time, you can almost see her, a woman in the fountain.

On the lower slopes of Kilauea, in the Wao Kele O Puna Rainforest–the only lowland tropical rainforest left in the U.S.–a Wyoming-based corporation has begun clearing roads through the forest and drilling for geothermal energy. For native Hawaiians, such actions are more than an insult to Pele. They threaten the forest itself, as well as centuries-old Hawaiian traditions and archeological sites. To stop the drilling, native Hawaiians have organized the Pele Defense Fund and forged alliances with a number of environmental organizations. *Photo by: Paul Chesley*

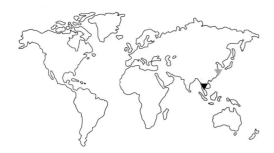

◄ **Bangkok, Thailand:** Rush hour never stops in Bangkok, especially at the intersection of Phet Buri and Phaya Thai roads. Lead pollution from automobile emissions is worse in less developed countries, where heavily leaded gas is still sold. Developed nations, however, must claim most of the responsibility for consuming fossil fuels. With only one-quarter of the global population, they consume four-fifths of the global energy budget. *Photo by: William Chan/Focus Stock Photo*

► **Wuxi, China:** Chinese cities were not designed for automobiles: Streets are narrow and parking is nonexistent. In this nation of more than one billion people, there are only five million vehicles, four million of them trucks. In contrast, factories produce thirty million bicycles every year. In Wuxi, the majority of people travel by bicycle because it is economical; it is also easy to pedal on the flat terrain. The sycamores, which are resistant to air pollution, have been pruned to provide shady canopies over the road. *Photo by: Volker Hinz/ Stern*

◀ **Osaka, Japan:** A bullet train leaves Tokyo Station. Japan's bullet trains travel 130 miles per hour, making the trip to Tokyo almost as fast as flying. The train is, after the human foot, the most energy-efficient way of moving humans about. The bullet train, not the supersonic transport, is the truly futuristic vehicle. *Photo by: Paul Chesley*

▶ **Prudhoe Bay, Alaska, USA:** The Trans-Alaska Pipeline runs through the heart of the last great U.S. wilderness. It divides North America's last Serengeti—the open tundra of Alaska's North Slope. Its service road has opened a pristine land of moose, grizzlies and wolves to more hunters and snowmobilers.

It need never have been built. Energy conservation could have saved all the oil it will ever produce. At the time of the pipeline's construction, for example, the Nixon administration was proposing a fleet of 500 supersonic transports. Those ear-shattering squadrons would have burned $10 million a day, just in the extra fuel required to make the difference between subsonic and supersonic speeds. That sonic boom would have consumed the entire two-million-barrels-per-day flow of the Trans-Alaska Pipeline, assuming it carried jet fuel instead of crude oil. In fact, it takes seven barrels of crude to yield a barrel of jet fuel. By making the sensible decision not to build such a fleet, we saved the oil of seven Trans-Alaska Pipelines. *Photo by: George Steinmetz*

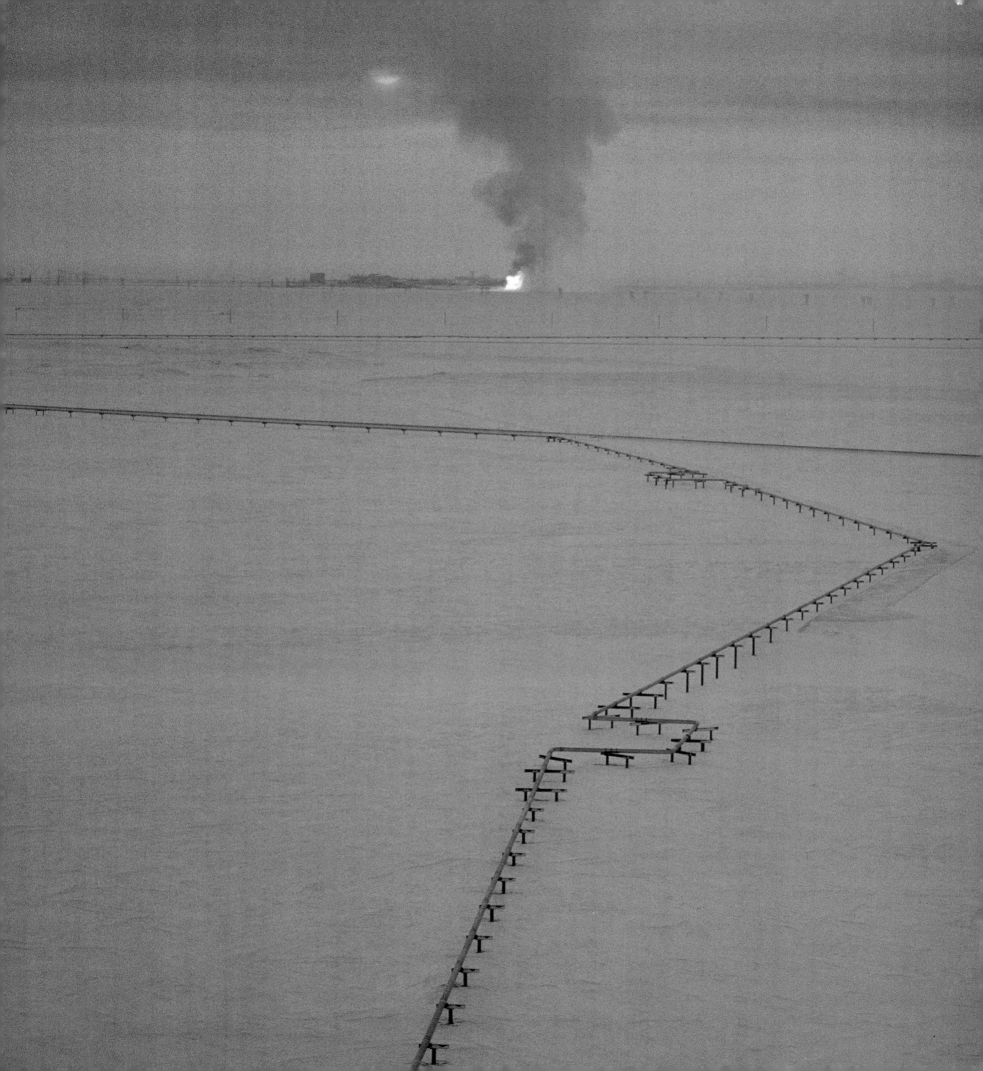

Environmental doomsayers grow irritating, sometimes even to themselves. Their prophecies can seem overwrought even as they write them. In the case of the Trans-Alaska Pipeline and North Slope oil, it is possible to compare prediction with history. The oil industry, in pushing for the pipeline, predicted smooth sailing for their product; environmentalists anticipated the opposite.

"If the pipeline is built, two million barrels of oil will daily move out of Valdez and cross fifty miles of restricted Prince William Sound waters before reaching the sea," wrote one worrier in 1974. "Sea captains are human and prone to error. Only one place on Earth, Drake Passage of the Antarctic, has rougher weather than the Gulf of Alaska. There is a lack of data on submarine pinnacles; the currents are strong and uncharted; there is an absence of suitable holding ground. Most of the North Pacific's storms are born here. Any collision or grounding of tankers, in this second stormiest of seas, could send oil shoreward. It will be unusually difficult oil to clean up."

The author of that text is the author of this one. Fifteen years after the prediction, the captain of *Exxon Valdez* retired to his cabin soon after setting sail, and his tanker hit one of those submerged pinnacles. The oil that washed ashore proved extraordinarily difficult indeed to clean up. Trouble and human fallibility are easy prophecies, of course. There is very little satisfaction in the I-told-you-so.

The March, 1989, *Exxon Valdez* disaster spilled eleven million gallons of crude oil into Prince William Sound. Contingency planning was woeful. Eighteen hours passed before chemical dispersants hit the water. More than 1,000 miles of shoreline were covered in oil. Officially, 1,016 sea otter and 36,471 birds died, along with unknown numbers of whales, porpoises and seals. Exxon spent $2 billion in a partial clean-up. The case will be litigated for years.

▶ **Prince William Sound, Alaska, USA:** Exhausted clean-up workers are ferried back to their quarters after the *Exxon Valdez* oil-spill. *Photo by: Natalie Fobes*

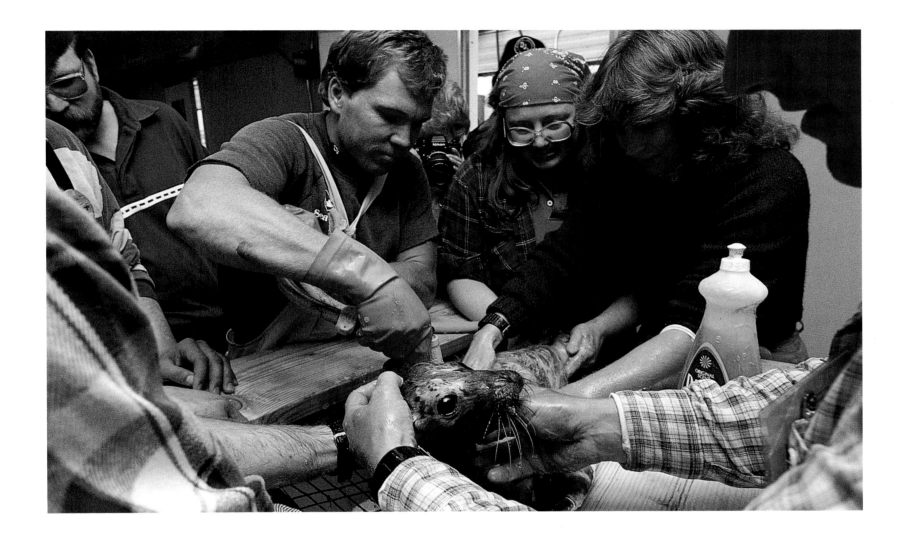

◄ **Prince William Sound, Alaska, USA:** After the *Valdez* spill, workers with high-pressure hoses steam-clean the shore of Naked Island. *Photo by: Anchorage Daily News/Gamma Liaison*

▲ **Valdez, Alaska, USA:** A sea-otter rehabilitation facility was set up to help some of the victims of the *Valdez* spill. Here an oiled harbor seal pup is cleaned. *Photo by: Natalie Fobes*

▶ **Alexander Valley, California, USA:** This geothermal plant, called "The Geysers," is the largest steam-field generating plant on earth, one of only two in existence. Steam from a natural "boiler" beneath the earth is collected by a system of pipes and sold to the local utility, which uses it to generate 1.3 million kilowatts of electricity. Subterranean steam is one alternative to burning fossil fuel. It is not likely to be a significant one. There are few sites available, and even in these the steam fluctates according to laws geologists are unable to predict. *Photo by: P.F. Bentley/Time*

Altamont Pass, California, USA: Wind energy is another alternative to fossil fuels. Windmills do not pollute the air; they simply steal a little of its speed.

Photo by: Stephen Johnson

Barstow, California, USA: Solar One, the largest solar thermal-electric plant on earth, covers 130 acres of the southern California desert. Its hundreds of mirrors rise with the sun, follow it across the sky and set with it in the evening. *Photo by: Peter Menzel*

▶ **Timbuktu, Mali:** Hamidu Mahamane watches over the solar panels of the women's cooperative of Tassakan. Solar power is the most promising of alternative energy sources. Any civilization that is to last on a planet of finite resources must learn to live within the budget of the local star. In rampaging through our stores of fossil fuels, we are using up our solar capital. In burning coal, we use sunlight that fell on the swamps before the times of dinosaurs. In burning oil, we use up the sunlight captured by diatoms of ancient seas and turned into petroleum. Mahamane and the women of Tassakan run their electric water pump with the sunlight that fell on Mali this day. *Photo by: Larry Price/Philadelphia Inquirer*

▲ **San Pedro, León, Nicaragua:** One of the crushing burdens on developing countries is the cost of imported oil. Nicaragua, like many poor countries, is desperate for alternatives. In 1988, members of the rural cooperative of San Pedro, trained by Terrasol, an organization of volunteer technicians, installed a simple system: one 40-watt photovoltaic panel, two 20-watt fluorescent lamps and a 12-volt, 90-amp-hour battery. The operating manual for the panel relies on pictures. The positive and negative connections are color-coded and fit only one way. To maintain fluid level in the battery, villagers need only add rainwater. Here, cooperative members clean the solar panel photovoltaic cells.

◄ The village of San Pedro now has its first electric light, which illuminates night classes for farmers. *Photos by: Lou Dematteis*

▲ **Barrow Creek, Australia:** In the 1987 World Solar Challenge, a 1,950-mile race from Darwin in the north to Adelaide on the coast, engineers proved that solar cars can go the distance. Among the participants were Ford, Nippon, Mitsubishi and General Motors, as well as college teams from Pakistan, Massachusetts and Missouri. The winner was GM's Sunraycer, which hit speeds of 70 miles per hour. In the future, we may be driving similar streamlined machines that take the energy of the sun and convert it into electricity. *Photo by: Peter Menzel*

▶ **Yosemite Park, California, USA:** The Yosemite Institute is a non-profit organization that brings students to Yosemite Park during the school week to learn about the natural world. Here, children have maneuvered through the "Spider Caves" in the boulders below Yosemite Falls. *Photo by: Galen Rowell/Mountain Light*

▲ **Finland, Minnesota, USA:** A red-capped boy meets a black-capped chickadee at the Wolf Ridge Environmental Learning Center. The mission of the center is to introduce young people to the environment. Classes and outings focus on topics like wildflowers, geology, painting, rock-climbing–and bird-banding, as shown here. *Photo by: Joe Rossi/St. Paul Pioneer Press Dispatch*

▶ **Anchorage, Alaska, USA:** A sick eagle exercises at the Arctic Animal Hospital. At least 150 bald eagles were killed by the *Valdez* oil spill. Many others were injured, and some of them were brought to the Anchorage hospital. After the spill came a banquet of carrion, and the eagles had eaten these oil-killed animals. Too much oil in an eagle's diet causes it to fly erratically. This bird, walking a straight line past biologist Karolann Longo, seems determined to pass its sobriety test. *Photo by: George Steinmetz*

▶ **Chitwan National Park, Nepal:** (following page) A mother rhinoceros and calf gaze at "eco-tourists" riding elephants in the dawn mist. Environmentally geared travel programs are bringing respectful visitors to threatened habitats–and hard currency to help fund conservation projects. The rhinoceros was on its way to extinction in Nepal, with fewer than 90 surviving, when the king of Nepal intervened. In 1972, he declared the rhino protected and converted his hunting reserve–the rhino's largest remaining habitat –into Chitwan National Park. Since then, the rhino population has quadrupled its numbers. *Photo by: Galen Rowell*

◀ **Mato Grosso state, Brazil:** A poacher displays skins of jaguars, margay cats and ocelots, most of which will be sold to dealers for fur coats. *Photo by: Martin Wendler/Peter Arnold Inc.*

▼ **London, England:** Climbers from Greenpeace hang an anti-fur banner from Harrod's department store. As the wearing of fur coats has come under attack, consumer demand has fallen. In 1990, Harrod's stopped selling furs. *Photo by: Katalin Arkell/Network*

▶ **Masai Mara Game Reserve, Kenya:** *Panthera pardus*, the African leopard, is on the International Union for Conservation of Nature and Natural Resources' Red List of threatened animals. It is one of a host of species headed for oblivion, unless homo sapiens mend their ways.

There is an eloquent sign in the Bronx Zoo that reads: "This red symbol calls attention to endangered species. Look for it around the Bronx Zoo. And think about what it means–the final emptiness of extinction." That warning marks, in a figurative way, the tree of this wild leopard. *Photo by: Stephen J. Krasemann/DRK Photo*

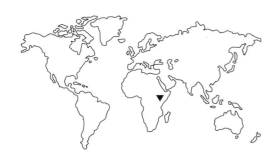

▲ **Kenya:** Twelve tons of elephant tusks, confiscated from poachers, burn in a demonstration of Kenya's determination to end poaching. In the past decade, the number of elephants in Africa has declined from 1.3 million to 625,000. In October, 1989, the Convention on International Trade in Endangered Species placed the elephant on its endangered list. More than 75 countries now ban ivory trade. *Photo by: Louise Gubb/JB Pictures*

▶ **Kenya:** A captured poacher stumbles in his march toward prison. Africa's war against poaching pits rangers armed with automatic weapons against poachers armed just as lethally. In Zambia, dozens of rhino and elephant poachers have been killed, along with police. In Kenya, more than 60 have died. Africa is the acid test of our determination to save wildlife: Humans there are dying so that elephants might live. *Photo by: Patrick Robert/Sygma*

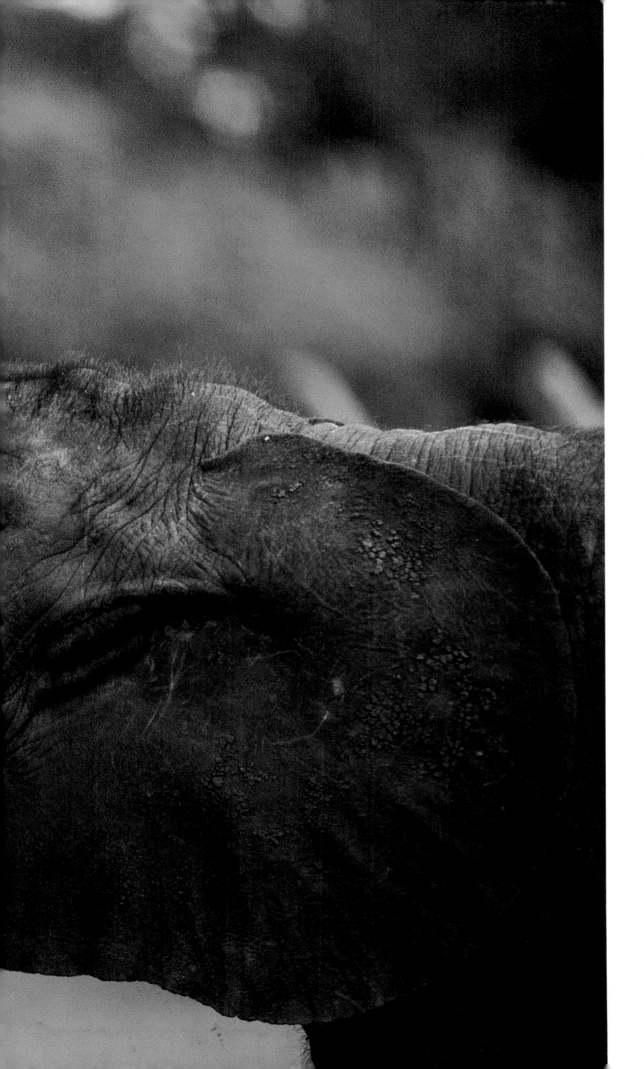

◀ **Nairobi, Kenya:** Since the elephant was classified as endangered in October, 1989, rangers in several African parks have stepped up their anti-poaching campaigns. At the moment, they seem to be winning. But Africa's "ivory wars" are likely to continue. Ivory is precious; Africa is poor. The ivory wars make widows of the combatants' wives, orphans of baby elephants.

The war has its Florence Nightingales. At the edge of Nairobi National Park, Daphne Sheldrick runs an animal orphanage. She and her workers care for young elephants and rhinos that have lost their parents. At the age of two or two-and-a-half, when they have gained sufficient tonnage, the young animals are returned to the wild. *Photo by: Rick Rickman*

179

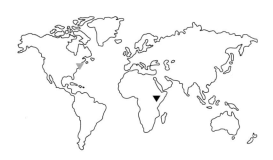

▲ **Mathare Valley, Kenya:** Throughout the world, people need to start reforestation projects. In Kenya, Wangari Maathai, the first Kenyan woman ever to earn a Ph.D., organized the Green Belt Movement in 1977. Her goal: to plant a tree for every one of the twenty-four million Kenyans. Maathai recruited 50,000 women to establish nurseries and then to help farmers raise the tree seedlings. So far, ten million trees have been planted. They are helping to hold back Kenya's advancing desert. *Photo by: William Campbell/Time*

▶ **Jamaica Bay, New York, USA:** On a Sunday morning in New York City, 15 4-H Club members clean up a beach in Gateway National Recreation Area. Here, Marcia Morales and Donna Duffin lift bags of trash. *Photo by: Monica Almeida/New York Daily News*

◄ **Mexico City, Mexico:** Is it a bird? Is it a plane? No, it's Super Barrio, Mexico's own environmental hero. Masked and in costume, Super Barrio appeared after the 1985 earthquake, which destroyed whole neighborhoods. Since then, this crusader, a former street vendor and boxer, has come to represent the poor people of the city's sprawling barrios. He campaigns against substandard housing, poor sanitation and air pollution. Super Barrio has become such a mythic figure that murals of him have popped up in the streets of Mexico City.
Photo by: Ricardo DeAratanha/Los Angeles Times

▲ **Guizhou Province, China:** Appreciation for nature has been an integral part of Chinese life and culture for thousands of years. Once a week, the children of this village near Kaili gather for a class in *ziran* (nature) to learn the secrets of flora, fauna and herbal medicine.
Photo by: Raphaël Gaillarde

183

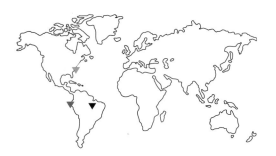

▲ **Altamira, Brazil:** At a meeting of managers of the Altamira Dam project, 600 Amazonian Indians representing 20 tribes made speeches and war dances to protest construction of the dam. Altamira Dam would flood 7,000 square kilometers of rainforest and bring 50,000 construction workers to Indian lands. One Kayapo woman swung her machete at the electrical company's chief executive, narrowly missing his head. The gesture was symbolic. The man took it personally. *Photo by: Claus Meyer/Black Star*

▶ **Washington, D.C., USA:** Earth Day 1990, held on April 22, was celebrated by 200 million earthlings in 140 lands. They thronged the Capitol Mall in Washington. They gathered–750,000 strong–in New York's Central Park. Fleets of kayaks and canoes held a "trash regatta" in Coos Bay, Oregon. Demonstrators presided over a "requiem for the earth" outside the Oak Ridge nuclear weapons plant in Tennessee. Saplings were planted in Vilnius, capital of Lithuania. School children in Morocco, Israel and Jordan participated in national clean-up campaigns. Rock musicians in Tokyo held a

concert (admission: 10 aluminum cans) on an artificial island reclaimed from garbage. Five thousand Italians staged a "lie-down" to protest car fumes. And the French formed a 500-mile human chain that spanned their country. Such worldwide activism is the key to saving the planet. *Photo by: Joanna Pinneo/U.S. News & World Report*

▶ **Galápagos Islands, Ecuador:** (following page) Peter Oxford, a naturalist-guide in Galápagos National Park, naps with sea lions. *Photo by: Galen Rowell/Mountain Light*

New York City, USA: Pablo Colón, an "urban pioneer" with the Bronx Frontier Development Association, hoists a future shade tree. *Photo by: Andy Levin*

Resources for Environmental Action

Organizations

The American Forestry Association: Directs Global ReLeaf, an action-oriented program aimed at improving the environment with community tree-planting and global reforestation projects. 1516 P St. N.W., Washington, D.C. 20005; (202)667-3300.

Citizens Clearinghouse for Hazardous Wastes: A national organization providing technical and organizational assistance to grassroots community groups fighting polluters. P.O. Box 926, Arlington, VA 22216; (703)276-7070.

Earth Island Institute: An international umbrella organization concentrating on deforestation, protection of dolphins, and environmental issues in Central America. Publishes a journal of international environmental news. 300 Broadway #28, San Francisco, CA 94133; (415)788-3666.

Environmental Defense Fund: A national public interest organization providing research, public education and legislative action in the fields of energy and resource conservation, air quality, toxics, land use and solid waste management. 257 Park Ave. So., 16th floor, New York, NY 10010; (212)505-2100.

Environmental Liaison Center International: An international coalition of non-governmental groups working on environmental and development issues. P.O. Box 72461, Nairobi, Kenya; (phone) 254-2-24-770.

Friends of the Earth: An independent global advocacy organization, represented in 38 countries, that works locally, nationally and internationally to preserve biological, cultural and ethnic diversity. 218 D St. S.E., Washington, D.C. 20003; (202)544-2600.

Friends of the River: A membership organization generating research, public education and political action to protect rivers in the U.S. Building C, Fort Mason Center, San Francisco, CA 94123; (415)771-0400.

German Green Party: One of the most successful of the politically independent "Green" parties around the world, providing a voice for environmentalism, as well as for the women's and peace movements. Die Grünen Im Bundestag, Bundeshaus, D-5300 Bonn 1; (phone) 49-228-16-2489.

Greenpeace, U.S.A: An organization that protects marine mammals and fights against toxic pollution, for nuclear disarmament and protection of the atmosphere. 1436 U St. N.W., Washington, D.C., 20009; (202)462-1177.

Institute for Food and Development Policy: A center for public education, internationally recognized for addressing the political and economic roots of world hunger and demonstrating how ordinary citizens can effectively help to end it. 145 Ninth St., San Francisco, CA 94103; (415)864-8555.

International Organization of Consumers Unions: An independent group that links consumer organizations in more than half the countries of the world and educates the public about the environmental consequences of consumption. 9 Emmastraat, 2595 EG, The Hague, Netherlands; (phone) 31-70-347-6331.

League of Conservation Voters: A national non-partisan political organization that works to elect pro-environmental candidates to Congress. 1150 Connecticut Ave. N.W. #201, Washington, D.C. 20036; (202)785-8683.

Natural Resources Defense Council: A membership organization that monitors government agencies, brings legal actions and disseminates public information about enviromental issues. 40 W. 20th St., New York, NY 10011; (212)727-2700.

Nature Conservancy: A national membership organization that purchases natural lands and cooperates with educational institutions and conservation agencies to protect ecologically threatened areas. 1815 N. Lynn St., Arlington, VA 22209; (703)841-5300.

Pesticide Action Network, North America Regional Center: Part of an international network of citizens' groups working to end the misuse of pesticides and to promote safer, more sustainable pest control. 965 Mission St., Room 514, San Francisco, CA 94103; (415)541-9140.

Rainforest Action Network: An international organization working in cooperation with other environmental organizations on major direct-action campaigns to protect rainforests. 301 Broadway, Suite A, San Francisco, CA 94133; (415)398-4404.

Renew America: A group addressing the need for increased natural resource efficiency, including renewable energy, water conservation and recycling. Provides publications for purchase. 1400 16th St. N.W., Suite 710, Washington, D.C. 20036; (202)232-2252.

Sierra Club: More than 50 chapters work on legislation and litigation, public information, publications, wilderness outings and conferences. 730 Polk St., San Francisco, CA 94109; (415)776-2211.

Trust for Public Land: A national organization working closely with community groups and government agencies to acquire and preserve open space for public use. 116 New Montgomery St., 4th floor, San Francisco, CA 94105 (415)495-4014.

U.S. Public Interest Research Group: A non-partisan organization that represents the public's interest in consumer and environmental protection, energy policy and governmental and corporate reform. 215 Pennsylvania Ave. S.E., Washington, D.C., 20003 (202)546-9707.

World Wildlife Fund: The largest private U.S. organization working worldwide to protect endangered wildlife and wildlands—particularly in the tropical forests of Latin America, Asia and Africa. 1250 24th St. N.W., Washington, D.C. 20037; (202)293-4800.

Zero Population Growth: A national grassroots organization that advocates population stabilization in the U.S. and around the world. Activities include citizen action projects, population education in schools, public policy advocacy and media campaigns. 1400 16th St. N.W., Suite 320, Washington, D.C. 20036; (202)332-2200.

Publications

Buzzworm—The Environmental Journal: A consumer guide to the environment with color photography and articles on sustaining the fragile planet. $18/year (6 issues) by subscription. (800)825-0061.

The Earth Report: A panel of international writers and scientists examines the most pressing current ecological topics—the problems, the actions being taken and what individuals can do to help. $12.95. Available in bookstores.

The Earthwise Consumer: A newsletter for finding organic, nontoxic, recycled and biodegradable products. $20/year (8 issues) by subscription. Box 1506, Mill Valley, CA 94942.

Everything You Ever Wanted to Know About Recycling: A free brochure from the Environmental Defense Fund, 257 Park Ave. South, New York, NY 10010; (800)CALL-EDF.

50 Simple Things You Can Do to Save the Earth: A concise handbook for everyday ecological living. $4.95. Available at bookstores or from Earthworks Press, Box 25, 1400 Shattuck Ave., Berkeley, CA 94709; (415)841-5866.

Gaia—An Atlas of Planet Management: A wealth of data, vivid graphics and authoritative text explaining the fragile interaction and interdependence of all living things. $18.95. Available in bookstores.

Household Hazardous Waste Wheel, Water Sense Wheel, and **Recycling Wheel:** Easy-to-use guides for the home. $3.75 each. Environmental Hazards Management Institute, P.O. Box 932, Durham, NH 03824; (603)868-1496.

Resource-Efficient Housing Guide: An annotated bibliography of books, periodicals and organizations with information on building materials, solar heating and other ideas for efficiency. $15.00. Rocky Mountain Institute, 1739 Snowmass Creek Rd., Snowmass, CO 81654-9199; (303)927-3851.

Shopping for a Better World: A guide rating the social and environmental performances of more than 150 companies. $4.95 plus $1.00 postage. Council on Economic Priorities, 30 Irving Place, New York, NY l0003; (212)420-1133 or (800)U-CAN-HELP.

State of the World ($9.95), **Worldwatch Papers** ($4 each), and **World Watch** magazine ($5 each, or $15 for a 6-issue subscription): These publications, designed by the Worldwatch Institute for government officials, journalists, students and concerned citizens, analyze environmental and economic issues from a global perspective. (Discounts for bulk orders.) Worldwatch Institute, 1776 Massachusetts Ave., N.W., Washington, D.C. 20036; (202)452-1999.

Stepping Lightly on the Earth—Everyone's Guide to Toxics in the Home: A four-page guide to doing housework without hazardous chemicals. Free with a self-addressed, stamped envelope. Greenpeace Action, 1436 U St., NW, Suite 201A, Washington, D.C., 20009; (202)462-8817.

Sponsor:

Eastman Kodak Company

Major Contributors:

Farallon Computing, Inc.
Hyatt Regency San Francisco
Pallas Photo Labs, Inc., Denver
The New Lab, San Francisco

Contributors:

Abaton
Barneyscan Corporation
Pan American World Airways, Inc.
SuperMac Technology
Symantec's Living Veideotext Division
Symantec's THINK Technologies Division

Our Thanks to:

African Wildlife Foundation
American Endangered Species Foundation
Ancient Forests International
Asamblea de los Barrios
CARE
Center for Investigative Reporting
Chesapeake Bay Foundation
Citizens Clearing House on Hazardous Waste
CODEFF
Dolphin Charters
Earth Island Institute
Environmental Project on Central America
Friends of the River
Greenpeace USA
Gulf Coast Tenants Association
International Development Exchange
International Org. of Consumers Unions
Lighthawk
National Geographic Society
Oxfam America
PANOS Library
Pesticide Action Network
Physicians for Social Responsibility
Pinnacle Type
Rainforest Action Network
Right Livelihood Foundation
Rural Advancement Fund International
Sahabat Alam Malaysia
The Baldwin Hills Crenshaw Plaza
The San Francisco Bay Guardian
The scientists and volunteers of the Farallon Islands
Tiger Tops Jungle Lodge, Nepal
World Wildlife Fund
Worldwatch Institute

Janine Adams
Sally Adams
Timothy B. Adams, Phd.
Sharon Ahern
Thomas Alcedo
Jeff Allen
Fred Allingham
Peter Almond
James Amanna
Robyn Anderson
Fred Anderson
Jon Andrew
Jesús Arias
Martin Arnould
George Atiyeh
Terry Backer
Michael Balick
Guy Barone
Super Barrio
Jeanne Bayer
Jim Beard
Lisa Berman
Kristin Berry
Pierre Bisaillon
James Blamphin
Saul Bloom
David Bolling
Bruce Borowsky
Miriam Boucher
Ellen Boughn
Bernard Boutrit
Jim Bredin
Bill Brennan
Marc Bretzfelder
Janet Bridgers
David Brower
Terry Brown
Sidney Brown
Bruce Brugmann
Kenny Bruno
Dan Budnik
Cindy Buff
Pablo Cabado
Anna Maria Caldara
Alejandro Camino
Woody Camp
Joseph Campbell
Robin Cannon
Pauline Capoeman
Ann Carey
Harvey Carlson
Joan Carroll
Kelly Cash
Aurora Castillo
Robert Caughlan
Bruce Chamberlain
Colby Chandler
Thomas Charkins

David Chatfield
Eddie Chavies
Linda Cloud
Bill Coblentz
Rodney Coggin
David Cohen
Pablo Colon
Tom Cook
Phil Cousineau
Lori Coyle
George Craig
Jack Crowley
Sheilah Crowley
James Curtis
Elizabeth Darby Junkin
Martha Davis
Linda Delery
Lou Dematteis
Ray DeMoulin
Chris Desser
Robert DeWitt
Michael Dickman
Chickie Dioguardi
Ibrahim Djibo
Peter Drekmeier
Mary Duffy
Kathleen Dyhr
Peter Dykstra
Denise Dykstra
Oscar Dystel
Gloria Eckert
Linda Ehrlich
Roy Eisenhardt
Sandra Eisert
Paul Ekins
Arturo Elejalde
Brian Empie
Dan Epstein
Christine Esposito
Larry Etu
Gail Evanoff
Kate Feiffer
Phil Feldman
Deborah Ferguson
Bill Fink
Prof. Tom Fleischner
Cary Fowler
Sara Frankel
Simon Frankel
James and Louise Frankel
Peter Fries
Peter Gabriel
Mary Jane Gallagher
Joy Gamble
Anabel Garth
Charlotte Gay
Gail Gelburd

Jean-Pierre Gernay
Debra Giannini
William Gilmartin
Paul Gipe
Nancy Goetzl
Michael Golait
Larry Goldstrom
Janet Gordon
Karin Grant
Bob Grant
Donna Gray
Claire Greensfelder
Lauri Gross
Brian Hajducek
Fred Hallett
Shelly Hamel
Ross Hammond
John Hartley
Robert B. Hawkes
Denis Hayes
Barbara Hedges
Diana Hembree
Mildred Jean Henderson
Dave Henson
Jack Hession
Bob Hirschfeld
Carl Hodges
Stephen Hopcraft
Dale Horstman
Bruce Howard
Georgeanne Irvine
Marjorie Isaacson
Wes and Dana Jackson
Ruth Jacobson
Tom Johnson
Cecil Juanarena
Darby Junkin
Greg Kaufman
Kathleen Kelly
Donald Kelly
Dr. Richard & Marianne Kelly
Richard D. Kelly, Jr.
Karolann Kemenosh-Longo
Donald Kent
Renee Kinsella
Dr. Edward F. Klima
Kristen & Dennis Korkos
Jaime Korkos
Nicholas Korkos
Péter Korniss
Mel Kreb
Michael Kressbach
Jeff Kriendler
Zorah Krueger
Tom Kunhardt
Sumiko Kurita
Elizabeth L'Hommedieu
Mr. & Mrs. Stuart Lamb
Marjorie Lamphear

Gilbert Lara
Stuart Laurence
Heidi Leabman
Rebecca Leaf
Billie Jeanne Lebda
Chris Lecos
Wendy Ledis
Marilyn Leland
Robert LeMere
Jim Lenfesty
Barbara Leslie
Chi Yoke Ling
Paul Lipson
Bela Liptak
Sharon Little
Ila Loetscher
Barbara Loren
Petra Lösch
John MacDougal
Judi Magann
Bedrich Magas Kusak
Mary Blue Magruder
Renée Mancini
Allan Margolin
Janet Marinelli
Kim Marshall
Gus Martin
Connie Matthiessen
Colleen McCarty
Ron McFarland
Loren McIntyre
Kim McKay
Tim McKay
Tom McMahon
Catherine McNeely
Dan Meer
Stan Minasian
R. Garrett Mitchell
Terry Morton
Ann Moscicki
Harriet Moss
Alexandra Mueller
Michael Murphy
John Nakata
Brad Nelson
Barry Nelson
Harold Nelson
Don Neumann
Carla Nicodemus
Chris Noble
Bernard Ohanian
Jim Olsen Jr.
George Olson
Mr. & Mrs. Art J. Ontko
Pamela Osgood
Dan Oshima
Steven Oualline
John Owen

Rusty Pallas
Sean M. Parks
Terry Parmelee
Michael Passoff
Barbara Peckham
Francisco Peña
Gregg Perin
Gabe Perle
Dale Perron
Tamra Peters
Bret Peters
Pat Peterson
Dr. E.W. Pfeiffer
Ray Pfortner
Jack Pichotta
Thomas Plaskett
Melissa Plemons
Mark Plotkin
Guy Polhemus
Larry Price
Darcy Provo
Michael C. Quinn
Daniel Quinn
Mark Rand
Robert Rattner
Toni E. Ray
Tracy Ray
Shannon Reagan
Tim Redmond
Gary Reed
Michael E. Reynolds
Beth Richardson
Rick Rickman
David Rinehart
Pamela Roberts
Geoff Rodareda
Barbara Roether
Scott Rosenberg
Clifford Ross
Laura Rowell
Mark Rykoff
Marianne Samenko
Ricardo Sampedro
Curt Sanburn
Carlos Sandino
Steve Sawyer
Aaron Schindler
Thomas A. Schneider
Mary Jane Schramm
Bob Seay
Cisse Sekouba
Bob Shanebrook
David Shaw
Bess Sherman
Stephanie Sherman
Judith Shmueli
Ahmet SibdialSau
Rada Simpraga
Gar Smith

Sally Smith
Jeffrey Smith
Rick Smolan
Tom Smylie
David Spitzler
Lee Sporn
Glenn and Rex Spray
Norm Steenstra
Dieter Steiner
Moli Steinert
Ginny Stevenson
Olivia Stewart
Mr. & Mrs. James Stites, Jr.
Lew Stowbunenko
Elizabeth and Larry Strain
Craig Strang
Michele Stueven
Michelle Syverson
Jon Tandler
Karen Teitelbaum
Lori Telson
William R. Thomas
David Tingey
Hector Tobar
Michael Tobias
Tom Tomaszek
Carl Tomoff
Darrell Totemoff
Jay Townsend
Alexander Kinghorn Turner, III
Nigel Turner & Heli-LA
Vito A. Turso
David and Cynthia Umali
John Valenzuela
Erik van Lennep
Janos Vargha
David Vigh
Frank Villalobos
Johanna Wald
Liz Walker
Joan Wall
Susan Watrous
Blue Watson
David Weir
Randall Wells
John Wells
Lisa Werenko
David Western
Jolyon Western
Marialuisa Weston
Jim Wheaton
Barry Wilson
Jeff Wise
Peter Wood
Claudia Wooldridge
Neil Young
Peter Zheutlin

One Earth Project Staff

President & Publisher
Bruce W. Gray

Editor
Ellie McGrath

Managing Editor
Kate Kelly

Design Director
Jennifer Barry

Designer
Kari Ontko

Writer
Kenneth Brower

Assignment Editors
Barry Sundermeier, Diana Reiss-Koncar
Susan LaCroix, David Carriere

Researchers
Susan LaCroix,
Diana Reiss-Koncar

Production Coordinator
John Clay Stites

Picture Editors
Sandra Eisert, *San Jose Mercury News;* George Olson, *Olson Photography;* Rich Shulman, *Everett Herald;* Anne Stovell, *Time;* George Wedding, Consulting Picture Editor, *Sacramento Bee*

Production Director
Lynne Noone

Production Assistant
Diana Jean Parks

Pre-Production Director
Stephanie Sherman

Research Assistant
Mary Beth Meehan

Copy Editor
Sara Frankel

Sponsorship Director
Cathy Quealy

Sales Director
Carole Bidnick

Publicity Director
Patti Richards

General Manager
Jennifer Erwitt

Business Manager
Peter Smith

Sponsorship Manager
Blake Hallanan

Staff Editor
Bill Messing

Film Traffic
Kathryn Yuschenkoff

Office Manager
Linda Lamb

Accounting Manager
Jenny Collins

Sales Coordinator
Maria Hjelm

Sponsorship Coordinator
Monica Baltz

Administrative Assistants
James Kordis, Scott MacConnell, Jill Stauffer

Editorial Consultant
Roy Eisenhardt, Director, *California Academy of Sciences*

Legal Advisors
Coblentz, Cahen, McCabe & Breyer, San Francisco

Dai Nippon Printing Co., Ltd.
Ryo Chigira, Fujio Ojima, Akira Ishiyama, Kikuo Mori, Mitsuo Gunji, Yoshio Akasaka, Yoshinori Katoh

Project Photographers

Monica Almeida, *New York Daily News*
Eric Lars Bakke
James Balog
Nicole Bengiveno, *New York Daily News*
PF Bentley, *Time*
Alan Berner, *Seattle Times*
Torin Boyd
Michael Bryant, *Philadelphia Inquirer*
Dan Budnik
Wayne Elliot Cable
Joe Cavaretta, *San Jose Mercury News*
Paul Chesley, *Photographers/Aspen*
Bradley Clift, *Hartford Courant*
David Cross
Ricardo DeAratanha, *Los Angeles Times*
Lou Dematteis
Jay Dickman
Don Doll, S. J., *Creighton University*
Dan Dry
Misha Erwitt, *New York Daily News*
Melissa Farlow, *Pittsburgh Press*
Enrico Ferorelli
T. Mike Fletcher
Raphaël Gaillarde, *Gamma Agency*
Diego Goldberg, *Sygma*
Bill Greene, *Boston Globe*
Judy Griesedieck
Stan Grossfeld, *Boston Globe*
Skeeter Hagler
Peter Haley, *Tacoma Morning News Tribune*
Bernard Hermann, *Les Editions Didier Millet*
Volker Hinz, *Stern*
Lynn Johnson, *Black Star*
R. Emmett Jordan
Ed Keating
Nick Kelsh
David Hume Kennerly
Kim Komenich, *San Francisco Examiner*
Péter Korniss
Steve Krongard
Jean-Pierre Laffont, *Sygma*
Sarah Leen
Andy Levin
Jonathan D. Levine
Barry Lewis, *Network*
John Marmaras
Richard Marshall, *St. Paul Pioneer Press Dispatch*
Stephanie Maze, *National Geographic*
Wally McNamee, *Newsweek*
Jim Mendenhall, *Los Angeles Times*
Doug Menuez
Claus C. Meyer, *Black Star*
Tomas Muscionico, *Contact Press Images*
Seny Norasingh, *Light Sensitive*
Randy Olson, *Pittsburgh Press*
Graeme Outerbridge
David Peterson, *Des Moines Register*
Joanna B. Pinneo, *US News & World Report*
Larry C. Price, *Philadelphia Inquirer*
Chris Rainier, *Photographers/Aspen*
Randy L. Rasmussen
Jim Richardson
Rick Rickman

Joe Rossi, *St. Paul Pioneer Press Dispatch*
Galen Rowell, *Mountain Light*
Brian Smith, *Miami Herald*
George Steinmetz
Patrick Tehan, *Orange County Register*
Ron Grant Tussy
Jerry Valente
Mark S. Wexler
Michael Williamson, *Sacramento Bee*
Michael S. Yamashita

Contributing Photographers

Katalin Arkell, *Network*
Richard Bangs, *Sobek*
Nina Barnett
Pablo Bartholomew, *Gamma Liaison*
Jim Brandenburg
William Campbell, *Time*
Dennis Capolongo
David Cavagnaro, *DRK Photo*
William Chan, *Focus Stock Photo*
Daniel Dancer
David Doubilet
Rainer Drexel, *Bilderberg*
Mark Edwards
Douglas Faulkner
Stephen Ferry, *JB Pictures*
Natalie Fobes
Charles Fox, *Philadelphia Inquirer/Matrix*
Bill Gentile
Gustavo Gilabert, *JB Pictures*
Ron Giling
Louise Gubb, *JB Pictures*
Chip Hires, *Gamma Liaison*
Kevin Horan, *Picture Group*
Helmut Horn
Stephen Johnson
Yuan Xuejun
Karen Kasmauski
J. Kyle Keener, *Philadelphia Inquirer/Matrix*
Sam Kittner
Stephen J. Krasemann, *DRK Photo*
Yuri Kuidin
Peter Lang, *Focus Stock Photo*
Frans Lanting, *Minden Pictures*
Susan Lapides
James Lerager
Renee Lynn
Mary Ellen Mark, *Library*
Peter Menzel
Reg Morrison, *Weldon Owen*
Ray Pfortner, *Peter Arnold Inc.*
Steven Pierce
Co Rentmeester, *Image Bank*
Patrick Robert, *Sygma*
Kevin Schafer
H.W. Silvester, *Rapho/Black Star*
Harald Sund
Martin Wendler, *Peter Arnold Inc.*
John Werner
Gordon Wiltsie
George Wuerthner

Anchorage Daily News/*Gamma Liaison*
NASA JSC/*Starlight*
Woodfin Camp & Associates